Beginning

at the

End

Beginning
at the
End

Finding Grace Through Faith
After Divorce

Sharon Elaine

Published by Three Poppies Enterprises
www.3poppiese.com

ISBN (paperback): 979-8-9915451-05
ISBN (ebook): 979-8-9915451-1-2

Book design and production by www.AuthorSuccess.com
Cover art by www.stock.adobe.com

This book is for every person who believes that they are too old, too broken, too shattered, too afraid, too guilty, too ashamed, too condemned, too late or too fearful to start a new life. Trust God. Begin to believe what His word says about you and watch your life change forever.

Contents

Introduction

I was sixty years old when my divorce was finalized. It took nine
months for everything to be officially over after forty years of hap-
piness/hell, joy/misery, faith/fear, hope/disappointment, and every
other contradictory emotion you can imagine. Everything was not bad,
but most of it was not good. When things were good, they were really
good, and I thought that everything had finally turned around, and we
were going to walk into the rest of our lives together. Then in the next
instant I would be back to wanting to run, never to return. I did not
know where I stood and what was going to happen from one moment
to the next. As anyone can understand, on again and off again takes
its toll on even the most stable person. But we were not stable people.
We were two broken people trying to make something work that never
should have been in the first place. We had nothing in common but
our brokenness. After all, being broken with someone was better than
being broken alone.

Years ago, I discovered that I had enough of the back and forth and
was ready to leave, but I ran into a glitch. I found out I was pregnant.
Now I had someone else to think about, to take care of, and to love
unconditionally. Still, I wanted to leave with the gift I had been given
to keep to myself, but I had nowhere to go with the blessing that God

had given to me to compensate for all my unhappiness. I had a family, but no family that would help me. So, I stayed and learned to protect myself by always expecting the next round of hurt, shame, guilt, and fear to come. By the time I left, I was shattered into a thousand pieces.

As I prepared to leave the chaos for the last time, I began to think about all the time I had lost. My youth is gone, and now I am starting my life over and alone. Like Job (Job 3:25), the thing I feared most came to pass. I started this relationship without a support system, and I ended it the same way. I reflected on Abraham, who was seventy-five when God called him (Genesis 12:4); and Sarah, who was estimated to be ninety (Gen. 21:1-7) when she gave birth to Isaac (no thank you, God). These great people of the Bible were older than I when God gave them their assignments. But more than age, I thought about not having the ability to see what was coming for me. Many times I was blinded by my perceptions of what I thought I saw in family, friends, co-workers, and my ex-husband. I tried to help people who were trying to kill me. Like Samson's blindness when dealing with the Philistines and Delilah (Judges 16:6), I used my physical sight to address spiritual problems. I have termed my spiritual blindness and weaknesses "The Samson Syndrome." I call it that because my eyes and own reasoning led me to catastrophe.

When I was a child, I saw the movie *Samson and Delilah* one Sunday afternoon with my dad. Samson's parents were visited by an angel who told them Samson must be raised as a Nazarene, set apart for God. He would deliver the Israelite people from the rule of the Philistines. The relationship between Samson and Delilah was accurate in that she did betray him to the Philistines. His head was shaved, and his strength left him. At the end of the movie, Samson was placed between two pillars that held up the Philistine temple that was filled to capacity.

Delilah came to Samson one last time to confess her love to him and to tell him how sorry she was that he had become a sport to his enemies. He told her he loved her, and he was going to destroy his enemies. Samson told her that she should leave so that her life would be spared. The Philistines gouged out his eyes, so he called out to her to make sure she left. Delilah remained silent. She did not leave and was killed with Samson and the Philistines. However, the Bible states that after Samson's capture, Delilah was not to be found. She took 1,100 pieces of silver from each Philistine leader and left. She was never mentioned again in the Bible. In his last act of strength and to complete his assignment, Samson killed more Philistines while physically blind than he did his entire life prior (Judg. 16:29-30). Samson was Israel's judge for twenty years (Judg. 16:31).

My family was Catholic, but I was never a serious practitioner. My father attended Mass every chance he got when he was not working on Sundays. My sister and I would go to Mass on Easter with my father. I went until I was about twelve. My mother and my brothers never went to church. I violated every rule, regulation, and religious practice in place that a Catholic should live by. I believed in God and Jesus, but I did not give them a place in my life. Like Samson, I ignored every rule regarding being a Nazarite, and I disregarded my Catholic roots. It cost both Samson and me time, that we never recover. Loving people who are incapable of returning love is costly. How fortunate are those who have never experienced unrequited love. Samson and I know the hurt of loving people who want our love for the purpose of manipulating us but have no intention of giving love in return.

I did the same thing with family members, people I thought were friends, coworkers, and my ex-husband. Like Samson, I was attracted to people who were assigned to take me out, whether they knew it or not. The deception doesn't start in a way that you would recognize. It is covert and very subtle, and before you know it, you see someone who is not there. Delilah knew what she was doing from the start, but I don't believe my ex-husband and I knew the disaster our relationship would become when we first met. I was looking for characteristics in him that he did not possess, but I saw that he could. I saw his potential and wanted to be the person to help him become what I needed, not necessarily what he needed nor wanted.

Delilah directly asked Samson three times about the source of his strength (Judg. 16:6-20). Three times she tested his answers. Three times the Philistines were there to seize him. One would think Samson would have sensed that Delilah probably did not have his best interest at heart and left with his hair intact. But Samson fell in love with Delilah, while she was only in it for the money (Judg. 16:4-5). So many times, I saw the signs, too. I had time to get out before the cursing, crying, anger, hurt, screaming, and lying got to the state of no return, but like Samson I stayed.

It is hard to be bombarded by people we love with constant requests for us to do something, give something, or say something that we know may end in tragedy. Delilah questioned Samson's love for her and constantly nagged him until he told her something that he never should have confessed (Judg. 16:15-16). How many of us have been in the same position? We've done something, given something, or said something that we profoundly regretted the moment it was done.

That is not love; that's manipulation. Someone who loves you does not use your love for them against you. My life was one consistent compromise after another because I wanted to prove my love to the man I loved. It's not hard for a broken nineteen-year-old looking for somewhere to belong and someone to belong to not see someone as who they really are because of who she needs them to be.

My ex-husband and I went our separate ways for about a year. I started dating someone else and he moved in with a former girlfriend. The guy I was dating proposed, and I took off from him like the foxes when Samson set their tails on fire because his father-in-law gave his wife to another man (Judg. 15:4-5). I did not want to be anyone's wife. I was in my early twenties and enjoying every bit of my life. So, my ex and I started talking again and ended up back together. If there were two people who should have kept going our separate ways, it was us. He could not get past me being with someone else and brought it up off and on. I pointed out that he was living with someone. If I could get past that he should be okay, as well. But he was not, and it followed us for the remainder of our relationship and through our marriage.

I had our daughter when I was in my late twenties, and our son a few years later. Since I did not know anyone who was happily married, I was not going to marry just because I was pregnant. He didn't want it and neither did I. What I wanted to do was leave with my kid. I had had enough of the accusations that I was cheating. But there was nowhere for me to go. My mom was embarrassed that I was not married. She did not care about my wishes; she cared that her unmarried daughter had a child and no husband. So, there was no help coming from her. My dad was on his deathbed, but he asked my ex to come to see him. They were in a room together for hours. When he came out of the room speaking with my dad, he was a different person. He never told me what was said. I asked my dad, and he did not say either. We still did not marry, but he was somehow kinder and gentler. For a while, we went back and forth, with one of us wanting to be married and one of us not wanting to. In the end, a demand was made to marry or leave.

Forty years is a long time to be stuck in a cycle. For years I did not understand why I allowed myself to be subjected to so much dysfunction. I have experienced some success in my life. I went back to school and obtained advanced degrees. I held prominent positions as an educator. I was in leadership, I was a mentor, and I led by example professionally. I assisted hundreds of students in getting their emotional, physical, and academic needs met. To look at me, no one could see how much I was suffering. My life was a train wreck. There was no peace in my home. I could not see how things would work out for me and my family. By the time everything was over, we were married, and our kids were grownups.

In my life, I have dealt with constant trauma. There was no plan for me to follow. I was alone. I walked through this part of my journey without the assistance of family, friends, and kids. Like Samson standing at the pillars, knowing that he had one last chance to complete his assignment, I had no escape plan. I had to do something . . . but what? Like Moses and the Israelites, I was in the wilderness for a generation. Forty years is a long time to wander around without a clue.

I could die in my own shame, condemnation, guilt, grief, and fears, or I could fight to regain what I had lost decades ago: myself. With God's help, and a lot of divine intervention, that is what I did. I will share with you some of the biblical scriptures in *italics* throughout the book that I stood on in my journey. I experienced my freedom by meditating on God's word. I learned how to receive healing for what no longer hurt. I set boundaries for allowing others to participate in my life and how I would participate in their lives, and you will, too.

I want to be clear regarding the obstacles you will face. It is an ongoing process. This book is about getting free and staying free by making godly decisions for your life. I could not get free if all I did was blame others for my participation in the nonsense that was my life. I had to take ownership of my part in the dysfunction. I had to fight to get my freedom and stand every day to keep it. I had to come to terms with the fact that I was not a powerless victim. You will battle blame, shame, guilt, fear, grief, and question your self-esteem. You must change your mindset to get through to victory. You must say what God says about you, about yourself. I came to terms with the fact that so many years had passed me by, but like Samson, I am going to make the latter years of my life greater than my former. You are not too old, and it is not too late to change your life for the better. We deserve every blessing, promise, provision, protection, and benefit that God has promised to us. You are fully equipped to do every good work (2 Tim 3:16-17), and you must battle all the thoughts that will tell you that you are worthless and it's too late to change your life. Change your mind, think the way God thinks, and it will change your life forever. Immerse yourself in God's written word.

This book is a deep examination of my life, which was never what I wanted it to be. My marriage was a part of it, but it was not the only problem that needed to be fixed. There were a lot of complications that came with my life becoming a disaster in general. There was so much that I did not know. I had no examples of a happy anything. My parents were miserable and so were my siblings. My thought was that I would stay with my husband until one of us died, but neither of us would leave. The plan was to stay in my unhappiness like my parents and just be resigned to life being wretched. I had no example of what marriage was, and certainly did not know what a happy one looked like. My parents just avoided each other. They never did anything together. There was no talking, no arguments, and communication was only used to get clarification regarding a want or a need. My parents were rarely in the same room.

My dad had a series of strokes over a ten-year period. My mom took care of him. She did not miss an appointment, a hospital visit, or forget it was time for my dad to take his medication. My mom followed every diet restriction and protected him from things that he wanted to do that would not be beneficial to his health, like driving or smoking. When my dad died, she was there with him. She lived for another thirty-five years after his death and never again dated or remarried.

I remember one year for their wedding anniversary, my dad asked my brother to get my mom a card and some flowers. My dad was confined to bed. My brother honored his request, and my dad presented the card and the flowers to her. My mom's reaction was indifferent.

There was no expression of disappointment or happiness. She did not read the card while she placed the flowers on a nearby table. There was not a "thank you" or any verbal or physical appreciation. I thought to myself, "What was that?!"

My dad was my favorite, and I was his, so I did not understand my mother's response. I found the answer to this question as I explored how I became the person I am and, in the process, discovered who I wanted to be.

This book will take you on a deep dive into your own journey of self-revelation to reveal the person you believed was lost or never existed. During your pilgrimage, you will begin to analyze the events that shaped your life. In the process, you will ponder the ebbs and flows of a myriad of feelings and emotions. You will laugh and cry, feel joy and sadness, and explore love and hate, along with disappointment and happiness. You will examine relationships in your life that mean the most to you and the role you played in shaping those relationships. The initial confusion regarding why things are the way they are will become clear.

There are obstacles you will face on your journey. Every minute of every day will be different. The highs and the lows will sometimes feel overwhelming. Guilt, shame, fear, loss, and grief will compete for your companionship on your expedition. You will go through the stages of grief, examine the way you trust, and learn to set boundaries. This is going to take place in layers to get you to the smallest cell of your core. You will be amazed at what you will discover about yourself. I had to battle and become someone I never thought I could be to get something I never had. You must do the same.

Acting as your personal coach, this book will help you assess where you are in your walk and provide you with a plan to move forward. You will discover your triggers, how to set boundaries, walk through forgiveness, and become aware of self-defeating behaviors to build your new life. I journaled daily for my first year. It helped me to process my feelings and my emotions. When my feelings ambushed me suddenly, I did not have access to anyone to talk out my feelings with me. Also, there were situations that I was not ready to talk about to anyone, so it was important that I had a way to work out my feelings. Talking on paper worked for me. For me, it helped to write it out. It freed me somehow. For you, it may be talking out loud to yourself or recording yourself. Do what you are comfortable with, but don't just think about your emotions or feelings without doing something with your thoughts. You should enlist at least one safe person to walk through this with you. For me, it was a friend I trusted who had already walked through divorce. For you, it may be a counselor or therapist, but it must be someone whom you trust.

At the end of the year, I was able to go back and review the progress I made. Looking at where I started and how far I had come encouraged me to keep going. You need to know that I could not work out forty years of feelings in a few months. It took two and a half years to walk through my journey. Thoughts still pop up, but I am equipped to handle them. You must decide how long the process will take for you. Don't rush the process. I could not have started my journey without my relationship with Jesus. He is our constant companion who will never leave us or forsake us (Matt 28:20, Heb 13:5). No matter how long you were married, divorce will have an influence on your life. This is something that you will need to work on every day. This is a journey, not a destination.

You will find scripture references throughout the book and at the beginning of every chapter. These are the main scriptures I used in my journey regarding the subject of that chapter. You will also see scriptures in parenthesis throughout the chapters; take time to research those scriptures. There are scriptures that you may see more than once, because I used those same scriptures to address more than one situation in my own life. Those scriptures may appear in the body of the chapter as well. Also, there are areas where I struggled more; those chapters will have more scriptures at the beginning of the chapter. The scriptures in the book are from the King James Version (KJV) of the Bible. Please find the version of the Bible that works best for you. It will give you additional insight to God's Word. Take your time and allow yourself to go through the process. I study the Bible to show myself that I am approved by God (2 Tim. 2:15). Walking with God is not a one-and-done. This is a life-long journey.

We have an enemy that is persistent and relentless. The devil may leave us for a season, but he will return as the Bible says he did with Jesus (Luke 4:13). The more of God's word you have within you, the better equipped you will be when the adversary comes. At the end of every chapter, it will be your turn to apply what you have learned to your own experiences. The questions are designed to be a guide to help you in developing your game plan for moving forward to your new normal. You should formulate your own questions about your situations that need to be addressed between you and God. This is an interactive walk with God that provides you with an opportunity to transform your life in ways that you never thought were possible. It certainly has been for me. Once you do, you will be amazed at the changes that begin to take place in your life. We all get one life. There are no dress rehearsals. It is up to us to do something with the life we have left. I don't know about you, but I have a bit of catching up to do. So, get your Bible, a journal, and a pen to begin a journey toward creating the plan for your new normal life.

CHAPTER 1

Learning to Adjust

But seek ye first the kingdom of God and all these things shall be added unto you. (Matt. 6:33)

"Giving thanks unto the Father, which hath made us meet to be partakers of the inheritance of the saints in light: Who hath delivered us from the power of darkness and translated us into the kingdom of his dear Son: In whom we have redemption through his blood, even the forgiveness of sins." (Colossians 1:12-14)

"Finally, brethren, whatsoever things are true, whatsoever things are honest, whatsoever things are pure, whatsoever things are lovely, whatsoever things are of good rapport: if there be any virtue, and if there be any praise, think on these things." (Philippians 4:8)

Getting adjusted to my new situation was a long process for me. I carried around so much baggage for so many years that I had no idea how to drop the bags. My mind was bombarded with thoughts about how I could be so stupid for so many years. I had given my life to someone who had no intention of loving me or providing for me. I constantly beat myself up for actively participating in the conditions I allowed. Shame, blame, guilt, and condemnation were my constant companions. I was so deeply wounded that only God could heal me, and for months I did not allow Him to do so. I was in survival mode, so I focused on the tasks that needed to get done. I wrote condemnation in my journal about myself and blamed my husband for this situation.

For the first few months, I was numb. I had to get used to being by myself after living with my family. I remember once I was leaving to run some errands, and as I was going out the door, I thought that I needed to let my family know where I was headed. I forgot for a moment that I was totally alone.

I kept myself constantly busy. I took on as many projects as I could, so I did not have to be in my apartment alone. There were times when I woke up in the middle of the night in a blind panic because I didn't remember I was alone in a new place. A month before my divorce was final, my brother died. Two months after my divorce was final, my mother died. They both died within three months of each other. This left me with the responsibility of my special needs sister while trying to make sense of my life.

My brother had children to arrange his funeral; my mother had only me. As you can imagine, attending my brother's funeral, arranging for my mother's funeral while taking on the welfare of my sister, and going through a divorce all at the same time became overwhelming. I moved my sister in with me for a few months while I found her an apartment not far from where I was living. I took the focus off myself to help my sister, which gave me some relief about my situation. While all of this was taking place, I began telling God how I felt and asking for help instead of complaining and blaming.

I took index cards and wrote out confessions to help me remember what God said about me. I recited them when I got up in the morning and before I went to bed. I found scriptures in the Bible about what I was feeling or experiencing that day. I carried my journal with me wherever I went. I left it in my car when I left home. I listened to sermons in my car about who I am in Christ. After several months of reading the Word, confessing the Word, and writing down my feelings, I started to feel a little less like a total failure.

Satan did not send strangers to destroy me. He sent people who were supposed to love me, protect me, support me, and provide for me. Satan will send parents, family, friends, classmates, bosses, co-workers, husbands, wives, and even your own children. He will send anyone he can to hurt and harm you. As I was working through my journey, I discovered that I gave everything I had to the people I loved because I loved them, but I did not expect them to love me back. They did not. The people I loved used my love as a weapon against me. Some were aware of the manipulation; some were not. I did not demand that they give anything back to me. I helped them however they needed it without thinking I needed them to give back to me in return. I did not think that I was supposed to want anything for giving whatever I could offer. I set no standards or boundaries for my own love and care.

In my past, I had constantly compromised myself to get the approval of my husband. There was a time, and for a long time, when I really loved my husband. I wanted to do anything I could to help him to see that we could get through anything together. But, instead of things getting better, they got progressively worse. The more I compromised to get him to want to live our lives together, the more I had to compromise. I was trying to get him to give something that he did not have the capacity to give. After our daughter was born, my focus was on being her mother. At that point, I wanted my kid and just wanted him gone.

Compromise was one area where I had to forgive myself. I did it all the time personally, but hardly at all professionally. In my profession, there are rules, regulations, policies, and procedures that I strictly follow. If there was ever a compromise, it had to be mutually agreed upon by all parties. Personally, I did not have any standards in place other than wanting to help my family. My husband and my kids received everything I could offer without any restrictions. I recall that as my kids got older, they would ask me what I wanted for my birthday. I always said, "I would like a clean house."

I did not know how to answer their question, because I had no reference for being asked what I wanted. I took anything that my family wanted to give, whether I wanted to or not. I taught my kids that I had no expectations, so anything they did for me was fine. I taught them how to mismanage my feelings, because I had no idea what I wanted for myself. Truth be told, all I really wanted was for the two of them to be with me as long as possible and know how much I loved and valued them.

Unfortunately, it took me a while to stop this trend. Even at the beginning of my separation, I compromised so that I would not offend my children. I allowed them to express their feelings without insisting that they understand what I was going through. I was hurting and alone. I would do almost anything to get my children to see me or even call. One day, I was reading my Bible and came upon this scripture in Isaiah 59:19: "When the enemy shall come in like a flood, the Spirit of the Lord shall life up a standard against him."

I had no standards and no boundaries, so I began to set limits on what I was willing to do in every situation. I started to value myself. I stopped taking anything anyone wanted to give me. I began to set boundaries that I would not cross or allow anyone else to cross. I began to believe that I was worth the effort to have people spend time with me. I started to believe what God said about me. I stopped allowing people to take me on an emotional rollercoaster. Instead of reacting, I journaled my emotions and feelings, which allowed me to obtain a sense of relief as I began to seek God first for help.

The disappointment I had in myself made it difficult for me to reach out to God. I felt like God was trying his best to help me, but I was so blinded by my desire to create a family with someone who did not want a family that I could not hear Him. As I continued to say what God said about me when a situation arose, I would say, "I can do all things through Christ who strengthens me." (Phil. 4:13).

Learning to adjust will be a vital part of your wilderness season. Your enemies may be in your own house (Matt. 10:36). People we love may not be as supportive as we would like them to be. Thoughts of disappointment and betrayal will attempt to take over your mind. Don't allow it. Spend as much time as you can in prayer. Pay attention to what you are thinking. Thoughts that are not of God do not belong to you. I often said aloud, "That's not my thought."

Be prepared for the onslaught of negative thoughts that will come to your mind. Do not wait until you need God's word before you know God's word. You must speak God's word only. Get God's word in you. Know who you are in Christ, and you will be able to fight the battles you face.

To get through this adjustment season, you will have to fight with yourself more than anyone. You will need scriptures to stand on when your mind starts to become overwhelmed with thoughts that try to overtake you. Write out your scriptures and recite them until they get down in your spirit. You must replace a negative thought with a positive scripture. You must speak the scriptures out loud, not just say them in your mind. Remember, faith comes by hearing the Word of God (Romans 10:17).

It is going to take some time. After all, I was with my ex-husband for many years, so it was not going to be a month or two for me to begin to say about myself what God says about me. Whether you have been married for a year or fifty years, give yourself time to process your thoughts and feelings. At the end of each chapter, reflect on thoughts and feelings that may not have been addressed in the questions at the end of the chapters. Make the time it takes to adjust to this new start for your life.

Learning to Adjust
Now It's Your Turn

Reflect on each adjustment you have had to make since your divorce. What is different about the way you have made adjustments?

If you had boundaries in place before your divorce, what were they and what do they look like now? (Be specific.)

What scriptures are you standing on in your adjustment season?

What are some thoughts you are facing that hinder your progress?

CHAPTER 2

Owning the Mess I Made

"There is therefore now no condemnation to them which are in Christ Jesus, who walk not after the flesh, but after the Spirit . . ." (Rom. 8:1)

"For he hath made him to be sin for us, who knew no sin: that we might be made the righteousness of God in him." (2 Corinthians 5:21)

"Christ hath redeemed us from the curse of the law, being made a curse for us . . ." (Gal. 3:13)

I want to remind you that most of my life I was not walking with God. When my husband became verbally abusive, he got back what he gave and more. If it was directed at one of the kids, he would receive triple the abuse from me. I fiercely protected my kids from everyone, including family. Believe me, their father was not the only one to feel my wrath. If I even thought you would do or say something that may hurt them, a mother bear or a lioness with her cubs did not come close to the attack you would receive from me. You would have been better off bleeding in open water with hungry sharks.

His behavior began to change mine (1 Cor. 15:33.) I became negative, verbally abusive, and cynical. I was mean to him but kind and understanding to everyone else. He noticed how I treated others and told me he wished I could show him the same kindness. I did not want to hear it. I did not show him kindness, because I felt as if I had to protect myself and the kids from him. I was fearful to be myself with him. If he was going to make me pay for wanting a family, I was going to make sure he paid for my pain. I had to own my part in my relationship that led to the failure of my marriage. In the beginning of the process, I could not see that I played a part. As I continued to see God in my walk, I began to realize that I played the most important part in owning the mess I made so I could move on with my life.

I was the victim that was constantly being attacked. In fact, I had empowered my husband to continue to place blame and condemnation on me without any resistance. I convinced myself that it was my responsibility to make our relationship work because I was the one who wanted it. Since it was not working no matter what I did, why should I be understanding and supportive of him? Then, I resented him for making me feel as if I had to change who I was to survive our marriage. I allowed him to put forth no effort to be kind to me and denied him what he was asking me to give. I blamed him for all the problems we had. I abdicated my responsibility of whether I could be happy to my husband. I was becoming someone I didn't like in order to survive our relationship. I am not mean, harsh, condescending, cynical, vindictive, and bitter. I started to become someone I did not recognize. I was lost. I thank God that He did not give up on me.

We are not good enough to make ourselves feel bad about something we want. Everyone can talk themselves into something that they know will probably not have the benefits they want. Rom. 7:21 tells us that even when we want to do good, evil is present. But if God is for us, who can be against us? (Rom. 8:31-32). Jesus will never leave us or forsake us (Heb. 13:5). Own up to what you have done, repent, and don't stay there. Only you can fix yourself.

If you blame and accuse yourself and others, you will remain the same and may lose what you have gained. In 1 Samuel 10, God appointed Saul to be Israel's king. By the time King Saul got to 1 Sam. 15, God had rejected Saul because of his rebellion and refusing to obey the instructions God gave him to destroy everything and everyone associated with the Amalekites. When the prophet Samuel confronted Saul about his disobedience to God, Saul made the excuse that he spared the best of the sheep and cattle to sacrifice to the Lord God. He also did not kill King Agag as God instructed. Instead of admitting he was wrong by disobeying God, Saul made excuses for his behavior. He did not own up to his mistakes and did not repent for them. He lost his anointing and place as king. God appointed David to be the next king (1 Sam. 16.) However, King David was seriously disobedient as well.

In 2 Sam. 11, David has an affair with Bathsheba, the wife of Uriah the Hittite. During the affair, Bathsheba became pregnant by David. David informed his captain of the guard Joab to put Uriah in the front where the battle was fierce. Uriah was killed, and David took Bathsheba into his palace as one of his wives. In 2 Sam. 12, the prophet Nathan delivered a message to David from the Lord regarding the murder of Uriah. Instead of David making excuses for his actions, he repented and confessed his guilt. Because of that, God forgave David and spared his life (2 Sam. 12:13). David was allowed to remain king because he owned up to his sins. Saul was removed because he made excuses. The Bible tells us, "*If we confess our sins, he is faithful and just to forgive us our sins, and to cleanse us from all unrighteousness.*" (1 John 1:9)

While Saul and David lived under the old covenant, we live under the new covenant given to us by the sacrifice of Jesus at the cross. We are covered by the blood of Jesus, and our sins are forgiven when we confess them to the Lord. It is important that we own our mistakes and ask for God's forgiveness.

There is so much pain in remaining the same. I came to the point where I had to stop the self-sabotage. I had to get past the point of my pain being a comfort to me. Blaming others made me feel better about the way I had lived my life. One day, the time came when I was ready to claim my life back and get to my healing. You will know when the time comes that you are ready to move on. At some point, you will want to stop the bleeding. Negative thoughts about how stupid you are, what a fool you are, and what an idiot you have been to love people who don't love you will probably bombard your mind. You will also likely focus on the time you have lost. You must fight to get past the self-condemnation that will surely come.

Ask God to forgive you and know that He will. I asked for God's forgiveness for my part in participating in the nonsense that was my life. Everything did not come to my remembrance at once, and I was grateful that it didn't overwhelm me. As things came to me through the Holy Spirit, I would repent and find scriptures to meditate on regarding my actions.

It is important that you pay attention to what you are saying about yourself, your situation, and others. Remember, you can have what you say (Mark 11:23.) Out of the abundance of the heart, the mouth speaks (Matt. 12:34.) Ask God to reveal to you what is in your heart and create a clean heart in you, and He will (Psalm 51:10).

Spend some time thinking about how you contributed to your situation (Rom. 8:1-2). Before you do, find scriptures so that you do not get into the habit of condemnation. Own the mess you made and move on. God will clean you up if you allow yourself to go through the process. This may be one of the hardest walks in your new season. This journey is designed to help you root out behaviors that need to be addressed before you move on to the next season in your life. There will be people who will try to condemn you, and thoughts may come back that make you want to condemn yourself. Everyone has some-thing they are working on or should be working on with God. As Jesus told the scribes and the Pharisees who brought the woman caught in adultery to Him, let he who among you who is without sin cast the first stone (John 8:3-7). Keep yourself from throwing stones at others and yourself. Trust God to get you through (Ps. 3:5-6).

Owning the Mess I Made
Now It's Your Turn

What situations in your life may have affected your responses to others?

Are you making someone else pay for your pain? Who? How?

What do you believe has been done to you? By whom?

What is your plan for taking authority over your reactions to others?

What is your plan for coming out of the blame and condemnation that you have about yourself?

CHAPTER 3

My Perception of Marriage

"There is a way that seemeth right unto a man, but the end thereof are the ways of death." (Proverbs 14:12)

"For he that soweth to his flesh shall of the flesh reap corruption; but to the Spirit shall of the Spirit reap life everlasting." (Gal. 6:8)

"And be not conformed to this world: but be ye transformed by the renewing of your mind, that ye may prove what is that good, and acceptable, and perfect, will of God." (Rom. 12:2)

Before I begin, let me make a disclaimer: I believe my parents did the best they could with what they had to offer their children. I do not sit in any kind of judgment regarding their parenting and especially their marriage. I don't know what they had to walk through to get to where they were. I lived in a house with a mother and a father. My mother did not work, and my dad always came home. He took care of his family. I loved my dad. He was the one person I never wanted to disappoint. He talked to me about things that interested me and life in general.

My parents knew of God, but we did not live in a godly home. My dad would go to church on occasion; my mother never went to church.

My older brothers and sisters attended Catholic school. I think that was my parents' attempt to provide more of God for their children than they had. I remember both of my parents saying to us things that God did not like or telling us God would punish us if we did this or that. We never got in any real trouble, no one went to jail, and we all tried to do what was right as we believed it to be. My mother kept our home clean and in order, made sure we were respectful kids, and gave us an example of how to get things done in the home. I learned how to repair lots of things by watching and helping my mother fix things in our home. My dad worked six days a week to provide for us. He taught me how to cook and encouraged me to do well in school. They both fiercely protected us from people outside of our home. They were not alcoholics and did not verbally or physically abuse each other. From my observations, their marriage was a one-sided relationship. My dad loved my mother, and she allowed him to do so.

Love was not a word that I ever heard growing up. My parents never told any of us that they loved us. There was never a clear definition. My parents approached it differently. To my mother, love was something to be ashamed to admit. I think she may have thought there was a weakness to it that made you vulnerable to others. To my dad, it meant providing for a family. My dad was different with his daughters than he was with his sons. The girls got encouragement, protection, and advice, while he was harsh to his sons. There were no hugs, kisses, or any other displays of affection in my home, ever. So, I'm not sure where I got the concept of love or affection.

We never saw our parents exhibit any kind of affection. I know experiencing affection did not come from them or TV or movies, because at the time I grew up, everything was rated "G." Married people on TV shows like *I Love Lucy* or *The Dick Van Dyke Show* were married couples who slept in separate beds. Also, there were no minorities on TV and very few in movies. I learned from misguided conversations with friends and the environments outside of the home. What I saw in my parents' home was responsibility for family obligations from my dad and indifference from my mother. As my siblings selected their spouses, my mother became alive. She spoke up regarding how she disapproved of everyone we all dated and married. No one was immune; they were all equally disliked. My dad only spoke regarding the men his daughters married. My parents had favorite children who were obvious to all the other siblings. My youngest brother was my mother's favorite, and I, the youngest daughter and the youngest of them all, was my father's favorite.

My parents did not divorce, but every one of their children did. My siblings' marriages did not last. My husband and I lived together for years before we got married. I had children, but I did not marry. As a matter of fact, getting married was the furthest thing from my mind. Before I found out I was pregnant, I had decided to walk away from my then boyfriend. I had grown tired of the one-sided relationship. He could not hide who he was any longer and I began to get some idea of who he really was. I was ready to move on. I wanted my children, but not him as a husband. I knew that getting married because I was pregnant was not going to work for either of us. Every married person I knew was either divorced, dealing with infidelity, or one of the spouses had some type of addiction. By the time I was two months pregnant, I had moved into my own apartment. My boyfriend was picking up those old habits that originally attracted me to him. I really loved the guy he presented to me while we were dating, but that person was an illusion. Still, I wanted it to work. I wanted to marry him, but "He" was not the person I believed him to be. He wore me down like Delilah wore down Samson (Judg. 16:16), and I allowed him to move in.

It was wonderful. I had the guy back with whom I had fallen in love. He was attentive, thoughtful, generous, and understanding, with a great sense of humor. I could not believe he was back. We went to Lamaze classes together, and he actively participated. Then it hit. After our daughter was born, the guy I had wanted to get away from came back. This time, I did not have the option of just picking up and leaving. I was a mom now, and that was the most important thing I had ever done in my life. He knew it, too. That's what changed. He knew that I had no place to go and no one to help me, so I stayed. I learned to make the best of a terrible situation. I took all the feelings of hurt, shame, fear, pain, and guilt and pushed them down deep inside me so that I could try to stay with someone who was not qualified to be a husband and did not even want to try to be. He was good with our daughter. As a matter of fact, he adored her. That helped me to stay for her. I didn't want her to be without her dad. I stopped caring for myself. I put everything I had into my daughter and did everything I could to keep the peace with the powder keg I was living with. While I was waiting for the other shoe to drop, I had our son and earned four degrees. That was my way of feeling as if I had some control over my life. It kept me occupied with something other than my kids and how wounded I was.

I did not know God for most of my life. I had no godly wisdom, no discernment, or any other godly knowledge that would have helped me to make better decisions about my life. In 2001, I started attending church with my kids and their dad. However, I was still not married. He was not interested in marriage, and neither was I. As I developed my relationship with Jesus, I realized that the way I was living my life was not in line with God's will for my life. I gave my kid's dad a choice. I told him he had to decide to leave the relationship or make the commitment to marry, but I was not going to live with him outside of marriage any longer. We married according to the world's standards and divorced twelve years later. For years, I made my husband and my kids my master, not God. Pleasing people will always lead to putting people over God. It will not benefit you. Prov. 14:12 says there is a way that seems right to a man but ends in death. I thought that if I got officially married, things would start to turn around for us. They did not. God cannot bless a lifetime of living in sin. There are consequences to sin. God called David a man after his own heart, but the baby he had with Bathsheba died, and the sword never left his house (1 Sam. 13:14; 2 Sam. 7-19). When you choose to live in sin, God cannot bless your life. He blessed me with children, but he could not bless the way I chose to live before Him. I chose my own understanding, not the wisdom of God. My ex-husband and I paid a price for the way we chose to live. I thank God for his grace and mercy, because even though we paid the price by the severing of our marriage, he blessed us with our children, whom we did not deserve. We lived to see our children become adults.

Our children did not know that we were not married when they were growing up. My husband and I lived like a married couple. I wanted to tell them, but at the same time, I did not want them to know. I did not want them to use what we did as an excuse for making the same mistake we had made. We decided not to tell them because we did not believe it would have been beneficial. As time went on, the guilt and shame I felt about staying with someone so dysfunctional who was not my husband became overwhelming. I didn't want my children to think it was okay to live the way I did. It was not what I really wanted for them. I wanted a better life for them than the one I chose for myself. I thought, "*Why put that shame on them?*" I still believe I made the right decision. When they found out, they did not handle it well. My daughter was more affected than my son. I cannot imagine what it would have been like to tell them as kids or teenagers.

It was shocking to me how much this affected my grown children. I was not prepared for the response I received from them. Their rejection of me was a complete surprise. They had witnessed the dysfunction I had operated in to keep the peace. They watched me do it all as they grew up in the middle of a disaster. I wanted them to have some type of stability growing up, so I stayed in a situation that I never would have allowed if not for my kids, since I had no family support and I did not finish college until after I had my children. When my husband told me that he wanted a divorce, our youngest child was in his late twenties.

I stayed and walked around on eggshells to keep the peace, and our children learned to do the same. I realized that my kids' hearts were broken, and they needed healing as much as I did. That shattered my heart. My kids were my only solace in this disaster. They are the only two people I ever really loved totally and unconditionally. There was a time in my life when the only way I believed there was a God was to look at them. There had to be a God, because look at what He allowed me to have. Look at my two wonderful gifts. I remember how I used to pray that God would allow me to live to raise my kids. I could not bear the thought of what would happen to them if I was not around. Their father and I fiercely protected them from as much as we could, but we should have protected them from us as parents.

I did not know how much I wanted to stay in this ungodly situation until I left. I was comfortable in my dysfunction and brokenness. I didn't have to think about anything anymore. I expected nothing and received the same. For all those years, I saw being married as the reason people did not stay together. It was the reason I was so against marriage for myself, because I thought the only way to stay together was to never get a worthless piece of paper, because one of us would end up with no intention of honoring the reason we were to be bound together by receiving it. In my mind, if I got married, I wanted to stay that way. I knew of no one who honored the commitment they made to each other. I knew a lot of effort went into the venue, the flowers, the dress, and the seating arrangements. The effort put into the marriage was nowhere near what went into the ceremony. But it wasn't the ceremony or the marriage license, it was all the hurting, dysfunctional, and broken people who surrounded me and fueled my misshaped view of marriage.

As I reflected on my view of marriage, the movie, "*It's a Wonderful Life*" came to mind. I thought about the main character, George Bailey, and his importance to everyone around him. After some trouble hit, George told his guardian angel that he wished he had never been born. The angel granted him his wish. I am reminded of his wife, Mary Bailey. Mary worked in the town as a librarian and was an old maid by the standards of that day. She never married, because George was meant to be her husband, but he was never born. I thought about how many people never met the person that may have been assigned to them because they were never born. They may have died before their time, miscarried, or even been aborted. I did not meet the person that may have been assigned to me. I'm not saying that I did not meet the right person because he was never born, I'm just thinking out loud about how many of us go through life never meeting the person we are destined to meet because they may have never arrived here on Earth or never crossed our paths because we were not listening to the signs that God was giving us. Even when we make the wrong choices, God never wastes a painful moment. What was meant for evil, he will make it good (Gen. 50:20). God always has a ram in the bush, and he will provide (Gen. 22:13-14).

Marriage is a blessing that God created for our benefit and is a part of his will for us to be in godly relationships with each other. It is people who distort His intended purpose. It is not up to your spouse or anyone else to make you happy. Only the love of God can do that. The joy of the Lord is your strength (Nehemiah 8:10). God was not opposed to me having a family. He wanted me to have one, but my thinking was malformed. My view of obtaining a family could not be blessed by God. When I made the decision that I would not marry under any circumstances, I was living outside of God's will for my life. When I began to seek Him and live my life as he intended, I began to see that my human effort accomplished nothing (John 6:63).

My misinformed reasoning for not getting married did not keep my relationship from falling apart. Coming to God's intended purpose for my life led me to be unequally yoked with my ex-husband (2 Cor. 6:14). He made up his mind that he was not going to follow God, and I was determined never to let God go. My perception of marriage changed to the perception of what God designed marriage to be for his children. As I closed the door on our relationship for the last time, this truth hit me like a bat to my head. I realized I had no idea what I was going to do, but somehow, I knew that God had my back (Exodus 14:14; Heb. 13:5), and I would be okay . . . eventually.

My Perception of Marriage
Now It's Your Turn

Where did you get your ideas/perceptions about marriage?

How did your ideas/perceptions about marriage affect your relationship?

Was anyone else affected by your decisions about your marriage? Who? How?

Why are you divorced? (Be specific.)

What part did you play in your divorce? (Be specific.)

CHAPTER 4

It's Complicated . . . But It's Not

"In those days there was no king in Israel: every man did that which was right in his own eyes." (Judg. 21:25)

"Every way of a man is right in his own eyes: but the Lord pondereth the hearts. To do justice and judgment is more acceptable to the Lord than sacrifice." (Prov. 21:2-3)

"It is the spirit that quickeneth; the flesh profiteth nothing: the words that I speak unto you, they are spirit, and they are life." (John 6:63)

I've heard testimonies given by people stating how grateful they are for the trials that God allowed them to go through. They said they were thankful for their experiences because they were better for them. I was never the kind of person who had to learn from experience. I was a compliant and obedient child. I did what I was told. If someone had advised me how to avoid such perfectly painful experiences that were implemented with such excellent execution, I would have listened to every word to avoid having my heart shattered. I was not the only one wounded; my ex-husband and our kids were also hurt. Knowing what I know now, I would have done anything that I could to spare them from their pain. They hurt me, but I hurt them too.

So many times, as I sat alone for months deep in thought, I asked God, "Why?" Why did I have to go through so much pain that cut me to the core of my soul? I was a good person and a good kid growing up. I never got into trouble and always did the best I could to be kind and respectful. "Why me, Lord?" I am not asking for anything extraordinary, just people to love me who were supposed to do that anyway because I am their daughter, their sister, their friend, their wife, and their mother. What's so hard about that? Why do the people I love want to hurt me? I'm trying so hard to help them to see how much they mean to me, yet I mean nothing to them. Help me to understand what I need to do so that they will care for me too. "What did I do to make this happen? How do I make it stop?" The rejection and the betrayal were so deep. It did not make any sense that everyone I love WANTED to play their part in my suffering.

The book of Judges (21:25), was instrumental in helping me to understand some of my why's. In the book of Judges, Samson, who led Israel as judge for twenty years, was dead (Judg. 16:30). Idolatry was rampant in the tribe of Dan. The Israelites and the tribe of Benjamin were at war because the concubine of a Levite was raped all night by men from the Benjamin tribe, and she died (Judg. 19:25-27.) The Levite took his concubine's body home and cut it up into twelve pieces and sent one piece to each of the tribes of Israel (Judg. 19:29.) This started a war between the Israelites and the tribe of Benjamin (Judg. 46-48.)

To understand the significance of the betrayal of this woman, you must know how the men of the Benjamin tribe got access to the concubine in the first place. An old man invited the Levite and the concubine to stay at his home with him because the men of the town were perverse (Judg. 19:20-21.)

The men of the town came to the house and began banging on the door, insisting that the old man give them the Levite man so they could have sex with him. The old man stepped out to talk to the men.

He begged them not to do such a terrible thing. He offered the men his virgin daughter and the concubine to let the men violate them however they wanted (Judg.19:24). When the men would not listen, the Levite pushed his concubine out of the door to the men, where she was repeatedly raped all night (Judg. 19:25-26). The men let her go at dawn. She went back to the house where the old man lived. When her companion opened the door, he found her face down, dead, with her hands on the threshold of the door. To add insult to injury, he told her to, "Get up, let's go" (Judg. 19:27-28). The concubine went back to the man who pushed her out, knowing that she would be violently abused, to protect himself. Too often, we go back to situations that are not safe rather than moving on to find help for our pain.

People do things that are sometimes unspeakable to protect themselves. These men were cowards for being willing to put women whom they should have protected in mortal danger. No, most fathers do not offer their daughters to rapists, and the majority of husbands don't push their wives out to men who will brutally violate them. But we do hurt each other all the time. The people whom I loved hurt me and I hurt people whom I loved. Most of it was not done consciously, but sometimes it was. Just like the concubine, I had no covering. I was not following God. I was the only woman in my family I know of who did not get married because she was pregnant. My dad never said anything, nor did he treat me differently, but now I understand that probably hurt him. The thought of hurting my dad is enough to make me want to drop to my knees in agony. But hindsight is 20/20. I didn't see at the time the impact my actions may have had on him. What I saw was everyone who married because they were pregnant had divorced after a few short years. I did not want that for myself. I was in this for the long haul. I thought that this way I would beat the odds, and at least we would stay together for life.

The scripture says that the people did what was right in their own eyes (Judg. 21:25). I certainly did what was right in my own eyes. When

I began to develop my relationship with God, I started asking all these "whys" about the hurt, pain, shame, rejection, and guilt happening to me. He could not protect me because I gave God no place in my life. I listened to my own advice. My misconceptions occurred because of a mindset that was based on my own experiences, not of God. I was thinking about life from my own perceptions. I began to want God to operate in my life, so I changed my mindset to think about life and make decisions from a godly perspective. God found a way through His grace and mercy for this ungodly, unwise, broken vessel not to be destroyed.

Everything about my life was out of order. I should have five children instead of two. I had two abortions and one miscarriage. I did not understand what I was doing when I aborted my children. I did not see them as children because they were aborted very early in the pregnancies. I had been told and believed that a fetus was not a baby. The fetus could not feel pain or any hurt. I had no idea that at the moment of conception that is a baby. It is life. When I had my first abortion, I felt inadequate to be someone's mother. My ex-husband (at the time my boyfriend) was not in a position to help me financially and I could not help myself. I knew that I did not have the strength to have my baby and give it away, and my boyfriend would not have allowed it, even though he was not equipped either. I thought the baby would be better off not being born than having me as a mother who had nothing to offer.

The next pregnancy was a miscarriage. I remember saying to my doctor that God was punishing me for having an abortion. I thought I deserved it. I did not deserve to have any children because of what I did. My doctor told me not to think that way. I would be able to have children and I should not have any guilt about what I had done. He said I had the abortion so early that nothing had been formed. And

I believed his lie. I had to believe him. I wanted to believe him. A few years later, I had my first-born child. When I learned that I was pregnant, I went to God as a heathen mother and gave my child to God. I made God a promise that day. I told God that if He would allow me to keep her, "I promise she will know you."

He kept His part of the promise. I struggled to keep mine, but I was determined to keep my word, not knowing how I would. I enrolled my daughter in Catholic school, and we went to Mass. That was all that I knew to do to keep my word. It would be years later before I began to keep the promise I made to God and give my life to Him, as well.

When my daughter was eighteen months old, I got pregnant again. This time was different. There was something wrong. My baby was not forming normally, and I was sick all the time. I was told that I would miscarry eventually. I decided to end the pregnancy. This time I did not want to end my pregnancy because I felt I would not be a good mother, but at the same time, I had an eighteen-month-old to take care of pretty much alone. That is not an excuse, and I'm not making an excuse. I'm saying that I felt like I made the best choice at that time. Four years later, I had my son. If I had God in my life, I could have asked Him to help me and my unborn child. My baby may or may not have lived. I will never know. I will never forget my three angels. But I can't dwell on what ifs or go there often. I don't want to give the enemy a foothold in my thoughts. I know I've been forgiven and someday I will see them.

This is hard for me because I really love everything about being with kids. I think they are wonderful. Every child should have parents who love and care for them. I could not bear the thought of having a child that I could not take care of because of my inadequacy. I was so mismanaged and discounted as a child that I could not imagine what kind of mother I would have been. I did not have an example of being a mother who loved a child just because he or she was mine. My children deserved more than I could give. I didn't want to do what I did, but I did it anyway. In Rom. 7:15-17, Paul talks about how we do the very thing we hate. This is an area where the enemy often attacked me.

The guilt, shame and condemnation were immense. The thoughts about how different my life would have been are real. At every turn, the enemy tells me that it's my fault that I don't have a family. He tells me that I destroyed my family by my own actions. I really must remember that I am holy, blameless, and unaccusable, and above reproach in my Father's sight (Col. 1:22). To win the battle you must remember that the Word of God is your weapon.

God was not first or anywhere in my life (Matt. 6:33). When Jesus is not the Lord of your life, the expectation should be suffering. Jesus took all our suffering at the cross; we must receive what has already been given (Isa. 53:5). But, if you don't know Him, you don't know that. I had the answers to my "why" questions after I began my walk with God. In walking around in the wilderness, the children of Israel went around the mountain for forty years. I walked around my own mountains for forty years. That's what happens when you are ignorant and disobedient. I learned that obedience is better than sacrifice (1 Sam. 15:22-31). The argument that I just did not know God is not a valid excuse. The apostle Paul states that when God created us, he put the knowledge of Himself in us. There is no excuse for not knowing God (Rom. 1:19-20). Let's face it; I did what I wanted to do, and as a result I was damaged, and I damaged people who I loved. The love of God would not let me go on suffering in my ignorance. Jesus saved me despite my wandering around in the wilderness.

In the beginning of our relationship, I did not want to say no to my ex-husband. For many of our years together, I wanted to please him. I compromised my standards so that he would stay, and we could be an out-of-order family. I knew what my standards were, but I willingly laid them down for the sake of pleasing him, and he allowed me to do it. In the end, I could not blame him for something that I had allowed. I changed who I was and my standards so that he could qualify. We drifted on and off the same page for the entirety of our relationship. He did try. He was there for the birth of our kids, and he named them both; he was there when my father died; he was there every time I walked across a stage to get a diploma; and he was there when I had a major surgery. He took care of me while I recovered. I could see that he wanted to do what was right concerning us, but he just couldn't hold on. The more I sought God for my life, the further apart we became. I thought that when I came to Jesus, things would get better. They did not. Things got worse between us. The times that we were on the same page sustained me so that the next time we were not, I had the strength to keep going. That was the way it went all the time we were together. It was an ungodly soul tie that kept me attached to a relationship that was never meant to be. I could not see that this was not God until I gave my life to the Lord. Before that, I believed a dysfunctional family was better than no family at all. This was not the plan and the purpose God had for me. God has a plan and a purpose for all of us to give us a hope and a future (Jerimiah 29:11). But I wanted what I wanted; not what God wanted for me. I got what I wanted, but I greatly suffered for it. God wants the best for us. We must reach out and take it. If I had not come to the place where I trusted God and let go of this ungodly relationship, it would have destroyed me.

Collateral damage is inevitable in divorce. Satan loves to bring people together to tear them apart. No one escapes. Kids are always in the middle of any painful decision their parents make. Our kids were adults, but they did not escape the repercussions of divorce. Other family members are torn away, as well. I lost my ex-husband's family when I left. He has siblings, nieces, nephews, and other family that I had a relationship with whom I no longer access. In fact, I was closer to some of his family members than I am to my own family. I had to make the decision to break free because I could not allow anyone to get between me and Jesus. He had to work on me with the help of the Holy Spirit, and I did not have the luxury of having someone else in my ear. I cut ties with friends that my ex-husband and I had in common. I went into isolation with Jesus. I had one friend who walked with me through the process of divorce and the loss that it brings, and another who kept me on track professionally while I went through it. I carried my own cross (Matt.16: 24-26). These two women were my only link to the outside world. I will always be grateful for them.

You will have to decide who can help you through your healing journey. There are some tough decisions that must be made. It is difficult to walk away from people we love to get the healing we need to become whole. Many times I was tempted to pick up the phone and call the people that I had been in a relationship with over the years when my ex-husband and I were together. I wanted them to hear my side; I wanted them to support me and tell me that I should have left long ago. I wanted them to hear how wrong he was and how right I was for finally leaving. I knew he was talking to people and probably misrepresenting the whole situation. But at the same time, I knew that was the last thing I needed to do. You will want to do it, too. You will want reassurance and support from friends and family. This is where your trust in God will be paramount. Whoever you select to help you walk through the process must be someone you absolutely trust.

You don't need someone who wants to gossip about the situation or exploit your tragedy. That is not the kind of support you need. I was not calling anyone, but they were calling me to "check" on me. We all have a belief system that we revert to when we are hurting. Your walk with God is going to be revealed in how you handle the negative press others want to provide to you. The question you will have to answer is who you are when the greatest tests that you may ever face come knocking on your door. There will be many opportunities for you to begin to listen to and speak words that do not line up with God's word. You must determine what you are going to allow yourself to be exposed to early in the journey. Who and what has your attention is what you will gravitate toward. Prepare for the war before the battles start.

Triggers are situations, circumstances, people, conversations, places, or anything that can take your emotions and feelings down a negative path to sabotage your progress and spiral you out of control. Everyone has different triggers. You must identify your triggers early in your journey to combat them before they come. For most of us, at the beginning of the journey, taking a stroll down memory lane is not a good idea. You will either remember all the things that made you want to stay or all the things that made you want to go. This will spiral your emotions out of control and prompt feelings you thought were long gone. There were days when my emotions were pulled in so many directions I did not know how I was going to get myself in order. I would be prompted sometimes by thinking about an activity that I used to do with my family or a movie I watched with my ex-husband. It would send me into a fury of feelings that triggered emotions that reminded me that I was going through this alone. Then my thoughts would turn negative, and doubt would rise to make me question if I was doing the right thing. Maybe, should, would, and could descended on me like a vice grip around my head. This is why identifying your triggers early will be vital to your journey.

Over the course of my life with my ex-husband and us as a family, I had quite a few triggers. Simple things like an outfit hanging in my closet that I wore to an event I attended with my ex-husband, a TV show, cooking a specific dinner, or someone asking me about him who had no idea we were divorcing, were a few of my triggers. I am really protective of family and friend photos. Those photos triggered me. I put away pictures of family, friends, and celebrations we had as a family. All of the photos of our vacations were put away, even the ones with just me and the kids, because he had been the one taking the photographs. Other things were souvenirs and gifts given to me over the years. Many times, I did not know something was a trigger until it happened. Pulling out the old photo album or getting back in touch with old friends may take you to a time that you are trying to overcome in your healing journey. Listening to music that the two of you listened to together may not be a good idea. Changing the way you think about these things will help you grow and overcome. You will be able to at some point, but by the time it no longer triggers you, you won't want to do it because you will be well on your way to a new you.

Your physical environment is important. Start by going through your environment at home and where you work to look for anything that may trigger you. It was easy for me to go through my environment because I moved out of the place where we stayed together. If you live with someone, try to get a room set up for yourself where you can go when you need to pull yourself together. I set my place up with all the new things that helped me to start my new life. It was easy for me to put furniture where I wanted and arrange things the way I wanted. If you need to rearrange your furniture, do that. My bedroom was my haven. I put scriptures on the walls, and bought new bedroom furniture and new bedding. Those things allowed me to feel good about my solitude between God and me.

Places can trigger you as well. Find new places to go. Try new foods and provide yourself with opportunities to talk with different people. If you like to go to the same places as your ex, go find something different if you can. In situations where you cannot leave or change, be prepared for people to approach you with questions. It will cause you less anxiety if you have a prepared statement for everyone and you stick to that statement. When someone asked me about how my ex-husband was doing, I would reply, "All is well." There were people whom I would run into occasionally who knew both of us. My brief statement would usually do the trick. If any other question came up, I would answer appropriately with as few words as possible.

Start new traditions you enjoy for yourself. At the beginning of my journey, I planned something that I looked forward to doing once a week. It was always something that I wanted to do but never had the time to enjoy. I looked for as much as I could participate in for free or at a discounted rate. Explore your city and other communities. Don't spend all your time working to pass the time. Work is good, but you are trying to create a new lifestyle, not replacing everything in your life with work to cover up pain. You must maintain a work-life balance. Think of something you may have wanted to try or someplace you've wanted to go and never had the opportunity to do it. Make plans for it. Find the good while you are passing through a difficult season. It is hard, but there can be joy in it if you look for it. Don't make it complicated for yourself, because it's not.

It's Complicated . . . But It's Not
Now It's Your Turn

Misconceptions about life produce an out-of-order way of thinking. What misconceptions do you have about your life? How are you going to evaluate your mindset to align with God's word about your life? Be specific about what the misconceptions are and the steps you will take.

One of the greatest sources of my self-condemnation is my unborn children. What is yours? What is your plan to deal with the condemnation and guilt that comes from this source?

Reflect. Who have you hurt in your pain? How were they hurt by you?

I made an alliance with my ex-husband to try to keep him instead of putting God first. What alliances have you made that put someone or something before God? Be specific.

What collateral damage has resulted because of your divorce?

Who can you trust to be part of your support system? Why?

What are your triggers and how do you plan to address them?

What is your plan to do some positive activities for yourself as you go through your journey?

CHAPTER 5

Band-Aids Can Not Fix a Shattered Heart

"He health the broken in heart and bindeth up their wounds." (Ps. 147:3)

"Wait on the Lord be of good courage, and he shall strengthen thine heart: wait, I say, on the Lord." (Ps. 27:14)

"And we know that all things work together for good to them that love God, to them who are the called according to his purpose." (Rom. 8:28)

The worst day for me when I separated from my husband was a Friday. That was the evening we spent with our kids. It was after school and after work, so I planned activities for us as a family. Usually, we watched a movie with our kids, and we picked up something for dinner that the kids liked. Sometimes we went out for dinner or watched TV shows that were family friendly. Our children were adults when I left and had their own lives, but I still missed us spending time together as a family. We did not spend every Friday together anymore, but we did get together as a family a few times during the month. I wanted to make my marriage work so desperately because I wanted to have a family. It was the most important thing in my life to me. I grew up in a family, but I was completely alone. Since I was not part of the family I was born into, I wanted to make my own.

My heart was like a stone from being so deeply hurt by everyone, but especially by my husband. I recall with total clarity the one incident out of all the times I was hurt that changed me to the point where I no longer cared about anyone but my children. I was not feeling well, so I went to get a full physical, bloodwork, and all. My physical included a gynecological examination. The doctor was a young intern who came in and asked me the usual health history questions. The blood was drawn, blood pressure checked, and the doctor performed a gynecological examination. He told me I would be contacted in a few days about the bloodwork, but to wait a few minutes for the results from the gynecology exam. He told me I could get dressed. He came back into the room and told me in a very matter-of-fact manner that I had an STD, and he was going to give me medication to treat it. I immediately began to protest that he had the wrong test result. I said he needed to redo the test because he had mixed up my test with someone else. I said to him, "I'm in a committed long-time relationship with one person, I do not sleep around. I am not cheating. That test is wrong. Go back and check the results."

At that response, this doctor, who looked like he was all of twelve years old, totally changed his demeanor I saw his compassion for me change his reaction to me. He looked at me with sympathy and care that he had not displayed when he first gave me the diagnosis. He put his hand on my right forearm, called my name, and said, "You have a sexually transmitted disease. It is called chlamydia. I am going to give you medication to treat it. It is curable. Take all the medication. I want you to make an appointment to come back in ten to fourteen days so we can do another exam. I am going to give you information about it. Please read it. If you have any questions, this is my personal contact information. Please call me at any time. If I don't answer, leave a message and I will call you back. Do you have any questions for me? Is there anything I can do for you now?"

After realizing he had just told a woman who had no idea that her husband was cheating on her that she had contracted a sexually transmitted disease, he left the room. I picked up the prescription and the information from the nurse on my way out.

I was dumbstruck. A stranger told me something that someone I had totally committed myself to did not have the courage to tell me. He had cheated on me and I had an STD. So many things entered my mind. How long was he going to let me go before he told me? With tears streaming down my face and uncontrollable sobbing, I thought he had to know about it. He must have experienced some symptoms. But he had said nothing. I glanced over the information the doctor gave me to make sure that it was curable and that I had the right treatment. I did not have the heart to read the information regarding how it could be contracted. But I knew. Our kids were out at a movie with my sister, so I could confront him when he arrived home. I did not say anything to him right away. I was still so stunned I couldn't speak aloud yet.

I started the conversation by asking him if he had something to tell me. He did not. I told him about my doctor's visit. I told him that I had been diagnosed with an STD, and I knew I was not sleeping around. He said nothing. I asked him how long he was going to let me walk around diseased without telling me. I told him that a doctor who looked like he was twelve had to tell me that my husband was messing around on me, and I felt like a fool. He told me that there must have been some kind of mistake, and the doctor was wrong. I knew at that point he was not going to admit anything that he had done. The fact that he had not tried to turn it around and say I was cheating on him, which is what he constantly did, was enough for me. He was caught but still refused to admit he had done anything wrong. I was outraged at his response. He still did not admit to any wrongdoing. I was humiliated, and really felt like a complete fool. I never thought he was cheating, let alone cheating with someone who could put both our lives in jeopardy.

Realizing that he was never going to admit to his actions, after I completely obliterated him with every ungodly word I could call him as a person, a man, and as a father, I said this to him, "You may as well keep doing whatever you are out there doing with whatever nasty whore you are doing it with. You brought me a disease and have no remorse about it. You won't even admit what you did. AIDS is rampant out here. What if you had given me something penicillin could not cure? We have kids, I need to be here to raise them. You are a selfish lowlife ##$%@!&%. I don't care what you do. Leave, stay, I don't care. But I do know this, and I want you to understand that I mean this, I swear to God that you will NEVER touch me again. It is a good thing that you are not affectionate with our kids, don't put your hands or your filthy lips on either one of them or I promise you I will have you arrested for child abuse. I don't trust you with my life or theirs. Get out of my sight. You are a disgusting piece of $#%&. Find somewhere else to stay. Go sleep with your whore tonight. Get out of my house." At that point, my relationship became the same relationship that my parents had. I instinctively knew what to do and what my expectations would be.

There was no resistance or argument to my request. He left on Thursday and came back Sunday night. I was grateful for the downtime. I needed to process my pain. I knew that we did not have the best relationship, but I did trust that he had my and the kids' best interests at heart. The trauma of the situation damaged me more than I imagined. I was not talking about him having an affair and getting someone pregnant, I was talking about the fact that he put my very life in danger. I could not get past that, and I never did. I kept my vow. We lived like roommates and business partners for the rest of our time together. I never allowed him to touch me again. Any affection I had for him as a lover was gone. The pain was too deep. I never looked at him the same. I did not trust anything he said. He had watched me take care of our kids, make dinner, go to work, clean our home, and everything else I did, and yet had no intent of telling me that he had exposed me to disease. When I finally left, there was nothing about him that I missed.

When I finally separated from my husband, the most profound experience for me was losing contact with my children, not because they could not contact me, but because they wanted little to no contact with me. I was devastated. No one could have anticipated that my children would respond to my leaving in this way. My mind was reeling as to what could have happened. I knew my husband would be belligerent, but I had no idea this would take place. I thought, "How could they treat me this way?" They were there as their father verbally abused me. They saw how he treated me with absolute disrespect. My kids witnessed how I was mishandled, marginalized, and mistreated. "What could possibly be going on here?" I constantly asked myself. I thought I would be supported and embraced by the children for whom I stayed in this godless union for so long. My heart had been cut, bruised, and battered over the years, but I was able to put bandages over the wounds and move forward while I bled through cracks trying to heal. This revelation shattered my heart into a million pieces as if someone put a bomb in my chest and pressed the detonator.

For several months I felt as if I was in a bad dream. I had one friend whom I spoke with about my situation, and I thanked God for her. I went to work during the week. On the weekends I planned things to do so I would not go into a deep depression. I knew if I did, there would be no one there to get me out. When I woke every day, I got up and dressed as if I would be leaving to go out. Otherwise, I would have been in my pajamas all day, which I did not allow myself to do. I spent my time watching sermons and studying God's Word as it related to what I was going through. This went on for about six months. I meditated on the scriptures and attended church on the weekend. Jer. 29:11 became one of my go-to scriptures. I knew God had a plan and purpose for my life, but I could not see it. Then one day, my son called and asked if he could spend the night at my place. This became a major turning point in my understanding of the reaction that I received from my children.

As I prepared my son's favorite dinner, he shared his thoughts about his father's and my separation. He revealed to me that he thought I could fix this. "Mom, you always made things work before with Dad. Why can't you do what you've been doing all this time and make it work now?" Finally, I realized that my children saw me only as a mother and their father's wife. It was my job to make things right for everyone, almost as if I was not human. I was supposed to be mistreated by their father, protect them from it, and not need or ask anyone for anything in return. After all, that's what I had done as wife and mother. I made it right for everyone to live their lives in comfort, because I took the hits from their father. My children saw me as the problem. Their father was being consistent. Dad was being dad. I was the one changing things and upsetting everyone's life.

My kids were comfortable in the dysfunction of our lives because they knew nothing else. My marriage was no example for my children to follow. I gave them the example I had seen as a child. I never let them see that I needed help. They observed that Mom didn't need someone to support her, care for her, and love her. Dad did not do it, and Mom took all the blows and didn't flinch. My children resented me for upsetting their way of life. Everyone was on their own and no one was equipped for it. I did not know that until I had this conversation with my son. Another chunk of my heart was wounded that day. I understood that I had wounded my children by not preparing them to handle the changes that needed to come, but I did not see them coming. I was not prepared, so I could not prepare anyone else.

In Tim. 4:16-18, Paul tells us about the first trial that he faced. He spoke about how everyone had abandoned him, and he stood alone. He asked God not to count anything against the companions who had once walked with him. But Paul said the Lord stood with him and strengthened him to preach to the Gentiles. As Paul discerned that his death was near, he knew God would deliver him from every evil work and bring him into the glory of God's kingdom. I was abandoned by those I loved, but I am not bitter. I love my children today more than I did then, but this love is different. It comes from my love for the Father. It comes from putting God first, so I know how to love better. God's love is love. I seek to love like Him.

As you walk through your own journey, you are going to discover that there are people around you whom you love and who are comfortable with your dysfunction. Life works for them when you continue to be an inferior version of yourself. I could not blame my children for not letting them see that I needed support long before I expected them to give it. The decisions you make about your participation in working toward mending your heart will start with people who wounded you. I started my road toward emotional healing with my son. He was the person closest to me who was willing to be honest with me and shared how he was feeling. It worked out for me because I wanted to help him as much as I wanted to help myself.

In this process, it will be important that you understand who hurt you and what specific actions or words hurt you before you can address the pain. Since most of the people who hurt or injured me were dead or I was unable to contact them, I used my journal and wrote letters to each person. The only people alive who I have access to are my daughter, son, and ex-husband. When I started to write letters to my children, I started out writing an apology to them for what I did to break their hearts. The Holy Spirit dealt with me and said, "This is about how YOU were hurt. This is not about what you did, but what was done to you."

I understood that until I confronted what was done to me, I would not be able to truly address what I had done to others. I am grateful that my son and I were able to talk to each other about our feelings without becoming offended. My conversation with my son started my walk toward healing.

Recognizing and addressing your trauma is significant. I discovered that my most significant trauma was my husband giving me a disease and not telling me. I had to deal with what I saw as the ultimate betrayal. I am still working on my trust issues with God's help. You must be prepared if you do not get closure from people who hurt you. It may never happen, and you must move on without it. My husband never admitted that he did anything wrong. He knew that he had given me an STD, and he never apologized for it. You may not get an admission of guilt or an apology. You must prepare yourself for that and be okay with it. Waiting for someone who is never going to apologize to you keeps your trauma in their hands. You are much too valuable to allow anyone but God to hold your future in their hands.

Prov. 4:23 says, "Keep thy heart with all diligence; for out of it are the issues of life." So often, we do not know "how" to keep or guard our hearts. We give our hearts to people who have no idea how to steward us properly. We begin to blame others for not giving us the affection, support, direction, or whatever else we need. As we blame others out of our wounded hearts, we begin to confess our hurt feelings and actions to others: ". . .out of the abundance of the heart, his mouth speaketh" (Luke 6:45). By not addressing my pain, I subconsciously wounded myself and allowed people I loved not to see how to properly steward my heart. I understood why I had to deal with myself first.

You cannot properly defend yourself with a broken arm or leg. Your range of motion is impaired. I lived my life with brokenness. I had a career that I loved, and I was able to help children and families and keep going with a broken arm, but I was not whole. I had access to God but not all the promises, protections, provisions, and benefits that Jesus sacrificed for me to have. I had lived, but it was a partial life. Putting Band-Aids on the gaping wounds in my heart allowed me to keep moving, but I could not heal. I didn't think I needed healing because I had stopped allowing myself to feel the hurt. Get your healing first so that you can be the example for those you love and show others how you keep your heart and how they can steward their own.

Band-Aids Can Not Fix a Shattered Heart
Now It's Your Turn

What significant trauma brought you to where you are? (Recall the details; be as specific as possible as you journal.)

What has been your reaction to your trauma?

What progress (if any) have you made to heal? If you have not made any progress, what steps will you take to move forward?

Who do you need to release for their participation in your trauma?

Think about who you can get to walk through this process with you. It should be someone safe. You may also want to consult a licensed Christian therapist.

You may never get an apology. How will you process that in order to move forward?

What is love to you? What does love look like to you?

How do you love God, yourself, and others?

CHAPTER 6

Forgiveness for All . . . Including Yourself

"For if ye forgive men their trespasses, your heavenly Father will also forgive you." (Matt. 6:14)

"Judge not, and ye shall not be judged: condemn not, and ye shall not be condemned: forgive, and ye shall be forgiven." (Luke 6:37)

"And let us not grow weary in well doing, for in due season we shall reap, if we faint not." (Gal. 6:9)

Forgiveness is the most important part of your journey. Without forgiveness, your plan for your new life will be severely hindered. You cannot get whole if you refuse to forgive. Jesus tells us in Mark 11:26 that if we do not forgive others, our Father in heaven will not forgive us. Forgiveness is an act of obedience to God. God searches the heart (Jer. 17:10). Forgiveness is an issue of the heart. Situations and circumstances happen to everyone. If you allow doubt and fear to creep in, Satan will have full reign of your thoughts and emotions. However, if you give your ear to Jesus and say what he says about you and believe what he says about you, the process of healing will begin.

How you respond and who you respond to will determine success or failure.

It was very difficult for me to forgive myself for the deception I lived with for the majority of my life. I had so many negative thoughts about myself that I had to overcome. I settled for what the people in my life wanted to give me instead of what I needed, because I didn't know what I needed to be whole. It was hard for me to admit that many of the difficulties I experienced were of my own making. Most of my unhappiness and disappointment I allowed. I put no demands on anyone. I poured out all I had and never received the refilling that only God could provide. There was a point in my life when I believed that since I had been so out of God's will for my life, I should just suck it up and take whatever the situation presented. I felt I had no value, no self-worth, and meant nothing to those who meant so much to me, so I should just take what I get and keep moving. I was there doing what needed to be done, but emotionally I was long gone. Because I was still getting things done, no one realized that I was only there physically. I bottled up my feelings and kept going.

After I gave my life to God, shame was one of the feelings I had to battle. I was so ashamed of what I had allowed to take place in my life. I told myself that it was too late for me to change my situation. I was living with someone and raising children outside of marriage. I'd had abortions and did not deserve the children I had. How in the world could I expect God to honor that? The person I wanted to walk through life with morphed into someone I didn't know. I believe I know how Jacob felt when Laban tricked him into marriage with Leah when he had agreed to work for seven years for Rachel (Gen. 29:18-26). My ex-husband became a person I would have never picked to go through life with, but I believed it was too late for me to do anything about that. We had two children, so I would stay and make the best of a terrible situation. After all, I deserved what I got because I did not follow what God said about my life. I highly respect the institution of marriage, but I did not see it as a practical way of life because everyone I knew had obliterated it so badly. I did not want to mess it up, so I thought not getting married at all would be the best way to stay together as a family. I was ashamed of my ignorance. I was ashamed of the disgrace it may bring on my children. They had done nothing wrong. How could I do this to them? I did not want anyone else to pay for my ungodly wisdom or my lack of discernment. My children did not know the situation they were born into until they were adults.

The close relative of shame is guilt. My condemnation was on another level. I felt guilty about every aspect of my life. I was guilty of living outside of marriage and having children in that situation, guilty about staying in an ungodly marriage, guilty about not living my life for God when I was younger, guilty about resenting my family for not giving me what I needed to feel loved. You name it and I was completely condemning it. I even felt guilty for wanting to be valued and loved. I did not believe I deserved to be valued because of the way I lived. Guilt is a terrible thing to live with. It talks you into believing that things out of your control are your fault. While I knew that I had no control over others' behavior, I equated everything to my willingness to live an ungodly life. The condemnation I felt would not let me see that I had been forgiven for all my sins. I believed that I should take whatever was given without complaint.

When you live in condemnation, it is easy to place shame and guilt upon yourself. I did not see a way out, even after I gave my life to Christ. Satan told me I was not worthy of being happy because of the way I lived. As I wanted to get closer to God, things became worse for me at home and at work. I was being attacked from all sides. I thought the decision I made to give my life to the Lord would stop the feelings of unworthiness, but instead, I was bombarded with feelings of inadequacy and fear. Then I read, "There is therefore now no condemnation to them which are in Christ Jesus, who walk not after the flesh, but after the Spirit" (Rom. 8:1). I learned that God would remember my sins no more (Jer. 31:34; Heb. 8:12). I learned that I was holy, blameless, unaccusable, and above reproach in my Father's sight (Col. 1:22). When condemnation led me to guilt and shame, I quoted these scriptures that told me who God said I was in His sight. If God says that about us, who are we to say we are not? Those thoughts will still try to come, but God's Word is our weapon to battle against the thoughts Satan tries to use against us so he can have dominion over our lives. We must have faith and believe the Word of God. "Faith cometh by hearing, and hearing by the word of God" (Rom. 10:17). Hearing your own voice speaking God's Word and speaking that word out loud is a very powerful tool against the enemy.

While I was blaming myself, I was doing a lot of blaming others as well. I blamed my ex-husband for lying to me and never admitting the damage he had done to our relationship. I blamed him for not fighting for us to stay together. I blamed my parents for not giving me a better example of what marriage should be. Blaming anyone does not work if you are serious about your healing. Blaming leads to unforgiveness, which will lead you to bitterness. Bitterness will lead you down a path you do not want to go (Heb. 12:15.) Staying in unforgiveness allows you to believe that you have the right to hold on to the hurt someone caused you. The person who hurt you may not know or care that you were hurt by their words or actions. My ex-husband knew he hurt me, but he would not acknowledge his actions. He cared more about protecting himself than he cared about what he did to us. That hurt me more than him cheating on me. He dismissed my feelings and made me feel worthless. From that point on, I felt marginalized and repeatedly rejected by him. I began to mirror his rejection of me back to him. If we are not careful, we may begin to emulate our hurt back on others. I imitated his rejection of me back to him. I was becoming someone who was backbiting, cynical, and hurtful to him. I did not care how harsh my words were to my ex-husband.

I needed to protect myself from him, and he understood my hurtful words towards him and respected me for using what he did to me back onto him. It was when I stopped using his tactics to defend myself against him that life got worse for me. He saw me as weak for following God's Word. He pounced on me like a lion on a gazelle. In the beginning, I could not defend myself because I did not know how to fight back using God's Word. I did not have enough of God to defend myself. I learned how to take the blows and push back by using my faith and what I knew about God's Word. Once I began to study more of the Bible, I learned how to respond to his hurtful words and actions in a Godly manner. His words were still like a sledgehammer to my gut, but scabs had formed over the wounds of my heart, so I was able to withstand the blows. However, I was far from being healed or walking in forgiveness.

Rejection is a powerful tool Satan uses to keep us in bondage. I can say without hesitation that I have been rejected by everyone in my family except for my dad. The people I have helped most have been the people who have shown me the most rejection. My first rejection came at age eight, delivered by my mother, who told me in so many words that she wished that she had never had me or my special needs sister. She probably thought I did not understand what she said, but I did. Rejection prompted me to do everything I could to please my children and try not to do anything to invoke my husband's anger. I became a people pleaser for my husband and kids. After a while, my people pleasing turned into entitlement by my family. I misunderstood my role trying to be a "good Christian" wife and mother. I became a doormat to my family. My ex-husband was quick to point out 1 Peter 3:1-2 to me. I was supposed to accept his authority over me. I was a new Christian, and I was hearing the same at the church I attended as a new Christian, so I allowed it. I permitted my ex-husband to heap his disappointment and disillusionment about his life onto me. It was not until a few years later that I learned his interpretation of that scripture was inaccurate. I did not recognize the types of rejection I was experiencing initially. It was years before I recognized the extent of it and the harm it had caused me. I know that my husband rejected me purposefully. After living with unresolved rejection long enough, the fear of being rejected started to operate in my life. My fear of rejection changed my personality, but not for the better. Keeping the peace became more important than anything.

Shame, guilt, condemnation, rejection, and fear are all reactions to emotions that I had to forgive myself for experiencing as part of my healing. It didn't happen overnight, but it did. I studied the scriptures to correct my mindset about who God called me to be and get an understanding of his Word (2 Tim. 2:15). Once I learned the truth about 1 Pet. 3:1-2, I also learned about 1 Pet. 3:7, that told me about how husbands should treat their wives. I can confidently say my ex-husband was not honoring me and did not care that his prayers were not being heard because he was not praying. I had to forgive a lot of lies that others had spoken about me that I believed about myself. When you know that you are not wanted by your mother, dismissed by your family, betrayed by your husband, and lied to by people you considered friends, there will be a lot to overcome. It was crucial to my healing to know and believe who Jesus says I am. I quoted scriptures that I learned and could meditate on when the lies I was told about myself tried to come upon me. I read the story of Ananias and

Sapphira (Acts 5:1-11). It significantly changed my response to how I permitted others' responses to lead my actions. I stopped allowing people to use the Bible against me by understating who I am in Christ. I no longer allowed my ex-husband to use the Bible to manipulate me. I did not have to follow his authority because he was not following God's authority over his own life. I got rid of the "ifs" in my life that told me that if I had only done or said this or responded like that, things would be better.

I've said this before, and I will say it again; It was harder for me to forgive myself than anyone. When we do not forgive ourselves, we tell God that the blood of Jesus was not enough to cleanse us from our sins. My ignorance concerning God led me to believe that what I did or said was so terrible that Jesus's sacrifice was insufficient to cover my actions, thoughts, or words. When I ran to God instead of from Him (1 John 1:7), I learned that he is faithful and just to cleanse me from all unrighteousness (1 John 1:9). Another thing I learned in my journey toward healing is that I categorized my sins. To God, sin is sin, and Jesus paid the price for all our sins. So, my fornication was not worse than lying, which was not worse than cursing, etc. I also would forgive based on what needed to be forgiven and who had committed the infraction. My forgiveness was a la carte. It was not real and did not last. If I was triggered, I would remember the infraction and that person went back into the unforgiven pile until something happened that I considered worse by someone else who triggered me. Then I would remember the offense that person committed, focus on them, and forget about the other person who reinjured me earlier. It was always someone's turn to be unforgiven or re-forgiven. As long as I was focused on why others deserved my unforgiveness toward them, I could not get to forgiveness for myself.

My heart was not ready to forgive. I had to prepare my heart for true forgiveness. I needed to hear and understand more of God's Word. I had to grow spiritually to forgive the way God forgave me (John 3:16). He gave his son for me and all of us so that we could understand the magnitude of what that meant. I had to comprehend what he did for me. My thoughts came to me in a practical way by looking at my son. I would never give my son for someone else to be free of anything. If I had to put my son on a cross so a multitude of people would mock and slander and disrespect his sacrifice, no one would be saved. Even if they did appreciate what he did, I still would not do it. We would all be in trouble if I had to give my son. But God gave the most precious, valuable gift he had. God gave his son so that I could keep mine. Jesus's faithfulness and obedience and his precious blood is the reason I am forgiven, who am I that I should trample His sacrifice to stay in unforgiveness toward anyone? After that simple analogy, I had no problem with forgiving anyone anything. Now, I was equipped to handle the ebbs and flows of walking in forgiveness. I could manage the triggers that used to send me into a frenzy.

I got rid of the lies others spoke over me and the ones I told myself. There were lies Satan told me, and he instructed others to tell me what I believed about myself that I had to renounce. I went lie by lie and renounced each one. I found scriptures to cover every lie and negative word that had been spoken over me, especially the ones I spoke over myself. I asked for God's forgiveness for believing the lies that had been spoken over me by myself and others. The vows I made in my hurt and pain had to be renounced, as well. My vows also kept me from growing in God. Making vows is a serious thing to do. Jesus tells us about the dangers of making vows (Matt. 5:33-37). I made "I swear to God" and "I will never again" vows that I had to repent for and ask God to forgive me. I asked the Holy Spirit to call to my remembrance any lies I believed or vows I had made so I could repent and renounce them (John 14:26). God has given us a promise that He will remember our sins no more (Isa. 43:25, 1 John 1:9).

In this part of my journey, I had to be very strict with what I said, what I did, and how I reacted to everything. I focused on what I wanted to have and what I wanted to happen. Any negative thought was dismissed with God's Word. I watched what I said. My "yes" was yes, and my "no" was no. If I was not sure about a request, I did not comment until I could give a yes or no (Matt. 5:37, James 5:12). If I said I would get back to someone, I did. I did not make any snap decisions or judgments. I allowed myself time to process my thoughts, which had never happened before. Spending time alone with God was a blessing. I began to hear his voice in my head instead of being bombarded with distracting thoughts. Paying attention to my thoughts, words, and actions was the best thing for me as I walked through this part of my journey.

This is an ongoing process in my journey. Thoughts are going to come and go. People are always going to have an opinion about you and seek opportunities to tell you what they think. Satan is a relentless but defeated foe. He is not going to stop trying to come against your mind, but we have the mind of Christ (1 Cor. 2:16). Meditate on God's Word. When the fear of who you were tries to come upon you, remember what God has said about you. You do not have the spirit of fear, but power, love, and a sound mind (2 Tim. 1:7). Be still and listen for God's voice (1 Kings 19:11-13). God is teaching our hands to war and our fingers to fight (Ps. 144:1). Ephesians 6:12 tells us that we are not fighting each other, but against ungodly spirits sent to plunge us into unforgiveness, doubt, and fear. However, the weapons of our warfare are not carnal but mighty through God (2 Cor. 10:4-5). Focus your thoughts on God's Word.

Remember, this is a journey, not a destination. The destination is heaven. I hate what Satan does to people and how we cooperate with him by being unaware of his evil intent for all of us (2 Cor. 2:11). My analogy for situations of blaming others who are unaware that they are being used by the enemy is that it's like a parent being upset with their infant for needing a diaper change. What sense would that make? It is the same to be upset with people who do not know they are being used by the devil. These people need our prayer. Jesus tells us to pray for people who curse us and use us spitefully. (Luke 6:27-28). When praying for someone, it's hard to walk in unforgiveness concerning them. I wish I could tell you I always think and feel how I should, but I don't. But now I know how to fight and win. Stop letting the devil live in your mind rent-free. Kick him out and keep him out by the blood of the Lamb and the word of your testimony (Revelation 12:11). Find scriptures that you can use to issue a counterattack against unforgiveness. Dig deep to forgive yourself and others. Be consistent in your prayers and confessions. Your new life with God depends on it.

Forgiveness for All . . . Including Yourself
Now It's Your Turn

Forgiveness starts with forgiving yourself. What are you going to forgive yourself for? Find scriptures that help you to forgive yourself for what you are experiencing. Continue to recite your scriptures out loud until they become part of you.

Whom do you need to forgive? For what? (Be specific.)

How did what happened affect you? (Be specific.) What scriptures will you stand on to forgive others?

What are you facing that will hinder your forgiveness walk (shame, fear, condemnation, blame, guilt, etc.) Write your plan for deliverance in the areas you are struggling.

The Holy Spirit may prompt you to go to someone and ask for their forgiveness. Pray and ask God to prepare you for the rejection and unforgiveness toward you that may happen.

CHAPTER 7

The Elephants in the Room: Age and Time

"So, teach us number our days, so that we may apply our hearts unto wisdom." (Ps. 90:12)

"But they that wait upon the Lord shall renew their strength; they shall mount up with wings as eagles; they shall run and not be weary; and they shall walk, and not faint." (Isa. 40:31)

"For I know the thoughts that I think toward you, sayeth the Lord, thoughts of peace, and not of evil, to give you an expected end." (Jer. 29:11)

"The Lord is not slack concerning his promise, as some men count slackness; but is longsuffering toward us, not willing that any should perish, but that all should come to repentance." (2 Pet. 3:9)

The word retirement is not in the Bible. Can you imagine Abraham, Moses, or Peter saying that they are retiring next year, and they have plans to golf every day or lay on the beach? Around the age of fifty, we start looking forward to the time we get to do nothing but what we want to do for the rest of our lives. Usually, our kids are adults, and we may have grandchildren we can spend time spoiling. Our culture accepts and even encourages senior citizens to ride off into the sunset to an existence of vacations, relaxation, and pet projects that somehow are never completed. Older folks have figured out something about life that led to regret of wasted time. Just when we have the wisdom to make better decisions about life, we may have health challenges, missed opportunities, or lack of financial resources to make the difference we need for stability in our later years. Our young people may not always have ears to hear what we have to say. The saying "youth is wasted on the young," is a real concept to those of us who are a bit more seasoned. In the Old Testament, the patriarchs and the matriarchs completed their assignments and went to their glory. However, in the new covenant, Titus 2:2-6, tells older men and women to teach the young people in the ways that they should go for the Lord. There is a new covenant to help one another. We are called to represent God as ambassadors for Christ (2 Cor. 5:20).

On every occasion I have attended where there were people I met for the first time, I have been asked, "What do you do?" It seems to be a question that leads me to define not only what I do for a living, but who I am as a person. As I began my walk, I asked myself, "Who am I now?"

I'm not a daughter, my parents are gone. I'm no longer a wife, I'm single. I am the mother of two children, and working with God's grace to build a new relationship with both of them. I'm a sister who takes care of a special needs sibling and have another sister I barely know. I'm an acquaintance to some and a friend to others. When I looked at my personal life, I understood why I always answer that question by sharing what I do professionally. Most people answer the question as I do, but we are a complexity of so many kinds of relationships to different people in the context of life. I had no other information to offer about myself except my professional credentials.

I lost so much time going in the wrong direction trying to determine who I wanted to be to myself and the people who were important to me. I've always been the person who said, "If you are still breathing, it's not too late."

But this time and in this situation, I was not feeling that way. I felt like my life was just a big waste of time. Who leaves everything they know to start their life over again and alone with nothing at sixty years old? What sense does that make? I didn't even have the career I worked so hard to get. I let it go to pursue another path a few years before my divorce. There was no precedent for my dilemma nor a mentor I could call for advice. I ran out in a vast ocean with no idea where the tide would take me.

I thought about my mortality. Who would remember me? What was I leaving here for my children? There will be no one around to tell my kids and my future grandchildren about what kind of person I was. Who would ever remember how pretty I was as a teenager and a young woman? I loved and respected my dad. I could hear him in my head saying, "Pretty girls don't stay pretty if they are stupid."

How stupid had I been? That statement did not help me feel better about the time I wasted and the youth I gave away with no thought. There isn't anyone to speak of the sacrifices I made in my ignorance. The adversary filled my mind with how worthless my life is and how forgotten I am. I would hear thoughts coming through my mind saying, with all the time I have spent here on Earth, I have nothing in the way of positive relationships because there is not a person who genuinely cares for me. I believed I missed my chance to get the things that are important correct. My thoughts told me I was too old, and it was too late to turn my life around and make a difference; that it was too late for me to be happy and too late to have positive, meaningful relationships. However, I rejected this negative train of thought and began to speak to myself what God said about me. I started to look to the Word of God for all the thoughts that tried to overtake my mind.

I must admit that when I began to study the Bible about age and time for women, there was not much there. I started down the road of discouragement. In beginning my studies regarding older women who overcome obstacles, there were Sarah and Elizabeth who were past childbearing years when they became pregnant and gave birth. Ouch, Lord . . . no thanks. But I know that my God is no respecter of persons (Rom. 2:11-16). I matter to God. He loves me and does not waste a hurt, because everything works together for my benefit (Rom. 8:28). If God could use a donkey, he could use me (Numbers 22:28). So, I silenced the negative thoughts that I allowed myself to think and began to listen to the Holy Spirit. I positioned myself to let the Lord lead me in the direction I should go. I stopped approaching my dilemma from an age, gender, and time perspective to remember that I am a joint heir with Christ (Rom. 8:17). I got off the rabbit trail the enemy wanted me to follow and held on to who I am in Christ. We all have an assignment; a purpose for being here. I did not find mine until later in my life. I still don't know everything about the purpose of my life, but I am learning line upon line, precept upon precept, here a little, there a little (Isa. 28:10). Sometimes we are not ready to handle situations that will prepare us for our higher purpose when we are younger. There are times we must go through circumstances that qualify us to grow into the plan and the purpose God has for us.

Everyone has heard of someone who obtained something before they were ready to manage it. I have heard of musicians, athletes, and family members who were scammed out of their fortunes because they trusted someone else to have their best interest at heart. They were either too young or too inexperienced. They had no understanding of the ramifications that trusting someone with no integrity would yield. I have experienced this personally when my elderly mother was scammed out of her home. Unfortunately, by the time I found out about it, my mother was dead and my special needs sister was swindled out of a home that should have been hers. It was too late for me to do anything legally to get the property back. The property had been transferred over for years without my knowledge. This brought back to my memory that I was in a family who had rejected me years ago, so I was not privy to the deception until after my mother's death. However, I was left with the privilege of taking care of my sister. I thank God that I am the one who gets to give the help and not the one who needs it. If I had been younger and not walking with God, I would have mishandled the situation. I did not have the wisdom to survive this hostile takeover. I would have greatly suffered as a result. We cannot see around the corner, but God can. I learned about this betrayal at a time when I could survive it and come out uninjured. I believe God will avenge us for the injustice and the theft that allowed the enemy to steal a family home from its rightful owner. Like the woman who went to the unjust judge and asked him to avenge her, I ask God to avenge me and my sister for what has been stolen from us. I realize that it is God's job, not my job. My job is to be persistent like the widow in reminding Him of what his Word says in Luke 18:1-8.

Gal. 4:1-2 talks about when a father dies and leaves an inheritance to his young children, the children are no better off than slaves until they become of age to receive their inheritance. 1 Pet. 1:6-7 tells us that we will endure many tests and trials to test our faith. Our faith is tested so that it can be perfected. As I said earlier, it took me a while before I began to follow God for my life. There were some things I had to learn. I had no idea what it meant to walk in the fruits of the Spirit (Gal. 5:22). I did not know what it meant to love because I did not know God. One of the fruits of the Spirit is peace. I had no peace in my life. Everywhere I went there was chaos. I knew about sacrifice, but not godly sacrifice. Long-suffering was what I lived by because that's all I knew. I was not supposed to complain, but that's what I did (James 5:9).

But God is a God of grace and mercy. He protected me in my ignorance because he knew what I was going to do from the beginning. God knew that I would come to Him when I had eyes to see, ears to hear, and a heart to receive Him. Jesus was there waiting. Many times, I was given discernment that I ignored because I did not recognize the prompting from the Holy Spirit. Jesus tried to warn me that I was going down the wrong road. It was the road I wanted; one that I chose. God respects our boundaries and choices. He will not force his will on us. He will step out of the way and let us have what we want. Remember, he let Abraham have Ishmael, Samson have Deliah, and David have Bathsheba. Each one of these situations had negative consequences, but God delivered these men from further calamity when they came back to Him. They were delivered from more consequences that enabled them to complete their godly assignments.

Only God can give us more time to complete our assignments. God told Isaiah to tell King Hezekiah to get his affairs together because he was not going to recover from his sickness and would die. King Hezekiah to pleaded to God and asked Him to prolong his life. God heard his prayer and granted him fifteen years (2 Kings 20:1-6). I asked God to give me back all the time I lost. I asked Him to return to me not only my time, but also every promise, protection, benefit, and opportunity that I had lost over forty years. I wanted all the tears, the hurt, and the pain to be paid for by giving me peace that surpasses all understanding. I asked God to renew my youth. I asked for everything that was stolen from me to be repaid to me seven-fold because the thief has been found (Prov. 6:31). It does not matter that I participated in my own destruction and deception; Jesus came to deliver us from it all. Jesus did not say that he would only save those of us who never messed up. The Bible is filled with imperfect people who accomplished great things. When God restored what Job had lost, he did not just give Job back what he lost but he also restored twice as much as Job had lost (Job 42:10).

Everyone has heard the expression, "Experience is the best teacher." I submit to you that it is not. Of course, when you learn by experience, you never forget the lesson, but it is an extremely expensive lesson. It cost me forty years. That is quite a few seasons of loss. Learning by experience takes valuable time. However, when you learn by godly instruction, you learn quickly, you still learn, and you don't waste time. Time is an irreplaceable commodity. If we don't depend on God, we may never recover. Only God can give you time and opportunities back. Ps. 90:12 tells us to ask God to teach us to number our days so that we may apply wisdom to our hearts. As a parent, I do not want my children to learn by experience. I don't want my kids to get hurt. I want them to listen to me when I give them advice and wisdom from all the years of experience I went through. Sometimes they listen to me, other times they do not. Still, I wanted to help, but I am not their best teacher. I have had to step out of the way and give their situation to God. I learned how to trust God with my children regarding the consequences that they may face. In the process, I learned how to stop crucifying myself. I put myself on the cross for every action and word I spoke. I was a lot more thoughtful about the advice I gave my kids than I was in following my own advice. But our children tend to do what they see us do while not listening to what we say. I gave good advice to myself, but I didn't follow it. Instead, I did not listen to what I now know was the prompting of the Holy Spirit to save myself the experience of doing whatever I was doing the hard way. I put my cross back on my shoulder and dragged it around for a few more years.

I was not ready to receive the things of God. My character had to be developed before I could move on with my life. My faith had to be developed along with my courage to live a godly life. I always thought I was brave, and I was able to live my life the way I wanted. When I could say what I wanted to say and do what I wanted to do without regard for what God wanted to do in my life, that was easy. I didn't have to put any restraints on my actions. I was comfortable with the strife life brought. God had to wait until I was ready to handle the assignment he had for me. I hit rock bottom, and he was waiting to pick me up. I learned the courage needed to resist hitting back in ways that would not cause harm, even when I was being hurt. The hardest thing to do is to let go so that God can take care of it for you. I never had anyone to take care of me, so the thought of Jesus taking care of me was a foreign concept to me. It takes faith to trust that God will take care of you. I didn't have any thought of God when I was younger, and honestly, I didn't want it. God waited on me to learn who I am in Christ and He will fight my battles so I can hold my peace (Exod. 14:14). God is longsuffering to give us a chance to get ourselves together (2 Pet. 3:8-9).

Society has told us that it's over for us when we reach the age of fifty, and we should accept the fact that life has passed us by. The life we live is based on the decisions we make. Do I wish that I had made the quality decision to make Jesus the Lord of my life when I was much younger? YES! But God, who knows the end from the beginning, knew exactly what would happen, how it would happen, and when it would happen. I do fight feelings that I'm too late, and that I missed out on opportunities and the life I could have had. I remind myself that while I may be severely delayed, God is always on time. He can place us where we should have been twenty years ago in a day. In 2 Kings 7, there was a famine in the land. It was so severe that the people were eating dove's dung, and donkey heads that sold for large amounts of money (2 Kings

6:25-26). The famine was so intense that women were eating their own children (2 Kings 6:27-30). God sent the prophet Elisha with a word that the next day people would buy flour for practically nothing (2 Kings 7:1). God sent lepers to tell the king about an abandoned camp with loads of food and supplies. God already had the answer to the famine. He turned the situation around in one day, using people whom no one wanted to go near. There is nothing He can't do. God can propel us forward so the time we mismanaged will not hold us back from what he has for us. God can give us back all the lost years in a nanosecond. Our job in this is to have faith and believe.

I am older. I've mishandled my time, missed opportunities, and made unwise decisions, but God has never left me. I do not believe things happen by accident or coincidence. To me, everything happens for a reason, and God does not waste a hurt (Rom. 8:28). I have no idea why it took me as long as it did to give my life to the Lord, and I may never know. All I know is that I am grateful that Jesus will never leave me or forsake me (Heb. 13:5). I'm grateful that I am still learning and growing in life. I have learned not to put a ceiling on my growth, but at the same time to use wisdom and discernment to look at every opportunity through God's lens. I will flourish in my old age (Ps. 92:12-14). I know that age does not mean wisdom, and it's never too late to make better decisions when you base them on biblical truths. Although some of us did not come to Christ early in our lives, it is not too late to make an impact for God's kingdom. Caleb was forty years old when he went to spy out the land of Canaan for the Israelites (Num. 13:30). Caleb announced that Israel was well able to possess the land from the occupants living there. When the land was divided among the Israelites, Caleb was eighty-five years old. He stated that he was as strong at eighty-five as he was at forty (Joshua 14:10-12). When God makes a promise, He keeps it. This is an encouragement to me that I am not too old, and it is not too late for me to receive every promise, every protection, every provision, and every benefit God has promised to me. I study to show myself an approved worker (2 Tim. 2:15).

Don't allow age, mistakes, or missed opportunities to keep you from what God has for you. With your age comes wisdom. Now that I can look back without all the clutter in my life, I can see how my mistakes happened. I could not see through the deception because I had no discernment, and when I could not see, of course, I was going to stumble. I seek God in every decision I make, no matter how small it may seem. I used to think that God had more important things to do than to be concerned about my day. I know now that is not true. He cares about everything that affects our lives. There have been times when I couldn't decide what to wear for the day. When that happens, I simply ask the Holy Spirit what he thinks, and I get an answer. God wants us to be in relationship with Him. When we want to develop a relationship with someone, we don't talk to them once a week for a few minutes. We call and communicate with the person often, sometimes more than once a day depending on the kind of relationship we are trying to develop. So, why would I think I can communicate with God once a week during a church service and that would be sufficient to have a relationship with Him? That is not going to work if you are serious about knowing God. If you pick up your Bible to carry to church and you never read it, you will not know your benefits.

People need us. They need your love, care, compassion, and, yes, your wise, godly counsel. Go get what you need to be whole and healed so you can be useful to the kingdom. It's not about us; it's about taking our place in the kingdom. We must get free of our past mistakes to help the people God has called us to get their hand in Jesus's hand. There are people assigned to you that if you don't step up and take your place in the kingdom, it will be hard for them. Of course, God will make a way for them, but it will cost them time. I am grateful that I had God and his love when tragedy struck my family. I was a grandmother for two days. My grandson was here two days before he went back home. His death shook me to my core, but it wasn't about me. My daughter lost her baby, her child. My prayers were for her and my son-in-law, for the strength they needed to get past this unseen tragedy. There was not much else I could do. I stand as an intercessor for them every day. Is it hard for me? YES. My friends and colleagues have grandchildren. Some were even born at the time my grandchild was born. I see the pictures and hear the stories about all the milestones their grandchildren are achieving. There are others who know my tragedy in this area, and they don't want to talk about their grandchildren with me. I encourage my friends to share their stories and pictures. It makes me happy that they are happy. Their stories are a blessing and comfort to me.

It's time for us as seasoned saints to step up and take our place. We need to get free so we can help others get free. 1 Pet. 4:18 says if the righteous are barely saved, what will the ungodly and the sinner do? You can't help your children or grandchildren if you are barely walking with God yourself. If you are struggling, go get the help you need to finally be free. After you do, the fight will not be over. You will have to fight daily to stay free. Our enemy is relentless. Satan will never stop using whatever and whomever he can to trip us up. He will convince us to speak against ourselves and to believe his lies, and he will work continuously to remind us of all the wrongs we've committed. We must remember who we are in Christ. Jesus took everything for us on the cross, so there is no need for us to crucify ourselves. We cannot help anyone if we are barely scraping by in our relationship with Jesus. Age is not an excuse. Loss of time is not an excuse. When I lost my grandchild, I needed outside help. I found faith-based godly counsel. There are times when you may have to reach out to get what you need to get free. I could not get through this one alone. I needed to talk with experts to help me so I could help my family. The Bible tells us not to despise small beginnings (Zechariah 4:10). This was a new beginning for me. I went to get the help I needed to break through my grief. I had never gone to get counseling for anything, even though I probably needed it years ago.

The Bible is our foundation for life. Our freedom is contained in God's Word. I need to stay strong in the Lord. I use other resources to support my understanding of God's Word. Whatever you are battling, you will need to get knowledge of your enemy. I listened to sermons, read books, listened to books on tape, tuned into podcasts, listened to discussions, and researched how others who had been through what I was going through obtained their freedom. To be free, be prepared to work for it. I am sure there have been times when God instantaneously delivered people, but that did not happen for me. Mine was not a sudden transformation. I learned to fight by battling my negative thoughts, feelings, and emotions daily. To get to peace that surpasses all understanding, I had to get through a war raging inside me and all around me (Phil. 4:7). We must fight to keep our peace. Anything or anybody that costs us our peace is too expensive. Eliminate whatever costs you your peace. Our kids and grandkids need us. My parents were lost, and so was I. Now, my children are in their rightful place, and I can give wise, godly advice to them if they want it and are willing to listen. They have been removed out of the place that only God should have. God has called us to a higher purpose, and we need to take it. We have family, friends, and a lost and dying world that needs our help. We need to know that when we walk in Jesus walks in with us. He has given us his authority to take the land. Like Mordecai told Esther, we were born for such a time as this (Esther 4:14). Let's rise up and take the land!

The Elephants in the Room
Now It's Your Turn

This one is all about you discovering the plan and purpose of your life. Take some time to reflect on what you believe about age and time as it relates to you.

What do you value about yourself? What have you learned about yourself that you did not know when you were younger?

What do you have to offer others that they will not get if you don't step up and take your place?

What do you do better than anyone else? How can you use that to help others?

How will you celebrate who you've become with age and time?

CHAPTER 8

Game Plan for Your New Normal

"Study to shew thyself approved unto God, a workman that needeth not to be ashamed, rightly dividing the word of truth." (2 Tim. 2:15)

"But be ye doers of the word, and not hearers only deceiving your own selves. For if any be a hearer of the word, and not a doer, he is like unto a man beholding his natural face in a glass: For he beholdeth himself, and goeth his way, and straightway forgetteth what manner of man he was." (James 1:22-24)

"For the weapons of our warfare are not carnal, but mighty through God to the pulling down of strongholds; Casting down imaginations, and every high thing that exalteth itself against the knowledge of God and bringing into captivity every thought to the obedience of Christ." (2 Cor. 10:4-5)

"Blessed be the Lord my strength, which teacheth my hands to war, and my fingers to fight." (Ps. 144:1)

When I came to the Lord for the first time, I was already over forty. I did believe in God, because I could look at my two darlings to know that there is a God, and he rewards us even when we don't deserve it, and I was grateful for that. God had so much more for me than just being a mom, but it took a few more years for me to be fully committed to having a real relationship with God. I wanted to know Him better but did not know "how." I started reading the Bible every day before bed, and then every opportunity I had to have a few minutes to myself, I read my Bible. I listened to every sermon I could about Jesus and the Holy Spirit. I studied God's Word as if I was taking classes for a degree. I could not get enough of learning about the Lord. Then one day, it happened. I had an encounter with the Holy Spirit while I was cleaning my house.

My prayer life became the most important thing I did for myself. I had my time alone with the Lord in the morning. I meditated on the Word throughout the day and before I went to bed. I took index cards and wrote scriptures on them to put in my bathroom, on my refrigerator, on the mirror in my bedroom, and on the door as I was leaving for the day. I also made a set to take with me, so I had them during the day. I saturated my thoughts with God's Word. When negative thoughts tried to come into my mind, I replaced them with a scripture about what God said about me or what I was dealing with that day. After about six months, those thoughts came less frequently. I always started by giving thanks to God for what he has done for me. When situations came up during the day, I had a scripture for them. I became a different person as my mindset changed. Phil. 4:8-9, Matt. 6:33, and Col. 1:22 became three of the scriptures I constantly quoted. They allowed me to think positively about others and myself. I still have the index cards and my time with the Lord all day. Some things are never going to change for me.

Coming to God and developing a relationship with Him did not happen immediately for me. In fact, I cannot recall any instructions from the Holy Spirit that came to me suddenly. I did not know how to listen for God. I had to learn his voice from mine, and that took some time. My new game plan came with battles I had to fight. The battles increased in intensity as I approached the end of the fight. Satan's plan is to have you give up right when you are about to win. You will have to fight, too. Satan is relentless and persistent. You will have times of rest, but remember that you are in a war for your very life. In that war, there will be many battles, and Satan does not fight fair. He comes to you when you are tired and battle-weary. It will be important for you to have someone who can encourage you during times of weakness. However, you will also have to learn to encourage yourself like David did (1 Sam. 30:6).

The more of the Word of God you have in you, the better you will be prepared for the battle. People will be placed in your life to hinder your walk. God puts people in your life, but so does the enemy. I had to remember that I was not fighting against the people themselves but against the way they were being used by evil to injure me. Be mindful of "who" you are fighting. This will keep you out of accusations and anger (2 Cor. 10:4-5). You will be tempted to speak against those who are speaking against you. Instead of letting your mind go to a negative place, think about what God says about the situation. Use God's Word to combat the enemy. You need to hear your own voice saying the Word out loud. If you are at home, in your car, in your office, or wherever you are, the more you can say the scriptures out loud to yourself, the faster they will get into your spirit. Speak only God's Word about situations, circumstances, problems, and people. It will help to keep anger and unforgiveness out of your heart.

Jesus commands us to love one another as He has loved us (John 13:34). Mark 12:30 tells us to love the Lord God with all your heart and your soul, and with all your mind, and with all your strength. Following this commandment keeps you from speaking negatively about anyone. It is necessary for spiritual growth. I cannot stress enough how important it is to not speak negatively about others. My mom used to tell me if I could not say anything good about anyone, I should not say anything. I did not know how profound that advice was until I started learning God's Word. There are a few other sayings I've heard along the way such as, "A thought unspoken dies unborn," and, "When you complain you remain."

I paid attention to what thoughts were going on in my mind. If something comes into your mind that you don't want, don't say it. Jesus tells us in Mark 11:23-26 we can have what we say if we believe when we pray, and that we should forgive anyone we have an offense against, so our Father in heaven will in turn forgive us. So, to have your prayers answered, love like Jesus loves, say what you want to have or want to happen, and not what you don't want to have or happen, believe you have it before you pray about it, and forgive people who have offended you. I will tell you that this was not easy for me in the beginning, but to receive what God has for me it was not an option.

I began to learn to trust myself. While learning, I realized why it was so important for me to keep my word. God tells us to let our yes be yes and our no be no; anything else comes from evil (Matt. 5:37). I had to believe myself when I gave my word or told someone that I would do something. I started to think before I gave anyone an answer about anything. The word "no" became a great word for me, and I used it often rather than saying I would do something I had no intention of doing. I stopped doing that to myself and to others. If I could not be honest with myself, how could I expect to develop trust in myself or others? Jesus tells us in Mark 11:24 that whatever we desire when we pray, we should believe we received before we pray, and we will have what we prayed. If I could not believe what I was saying about the little things, how could I believe about big things? If I am lying to myself, how can I trust myself or expect anyone to trust me? Prov. 6:16-19 tells us the seven things that are an abomination to God, one of which is a lying tongue. If I lie to myself and others, I cannot expect real trust to come to me or give to others. When I said what God said about a situation and spoke the truth about what I was or was not willing to do, my trust started to build.

Rebuilding relationships in which there is broken trust takes time. It is so easy to lose someone's trust but so difficult to rebuild it. No one wants to be hurt, so we guard our hearts. Trust was one of the most difficult aspects of my walk with God; even more difficult for me than forgiveness. Everyone whom I had ever trusted betrayed me, so it took me some time to develop spiritual discernment to know who I could trust. If not for discernment, I would not have shared anything with my friend who helped me through my darkest hours because I would have felt that she was going to betray me too. People we have hurt may have a hard time trusting us again. There are people whom I will never trust again, and perhaps there are also people who will never trust me again. When you want to rebuild a relationship with someone, you need to understand that you broke their trust, and as a consequence they may do everything they can to protect themselves from being reinjured. Depending on how deep the hurt is, that may mean that they want no contact with you. That may be hard for you depending on the relationship you are working to repair. If it is a parent, a child, or a sibling, it can be especially difficult. After all, it's hard to walk away from the family you love, regardless of the pain they may have caused you. To help me through this process, I started journaling.

I vented in my journal to keep me from speaking out in anger against a situation or a person. You are going to have to deal with any anger you have about your circumstance somehow, and writing your feelings out in your journal is a good way to handle your emotions. I didn't try to act as if I didn't have feelings. I spoke about my hurt, disappointment, happiness, joy, and all my thoughts went in that journal. It was my way of getting free without injuring myself or anyone. In the beginning, I did not have a set time for writing in my journal. I carried it with me for the first year after I left my marriage and for the first year of my divorce. After that, I wrote in the evening after work or before bed. I talked to God in my journal. I felt like he was there with me as I wrote to process my day. This kept me out of trouble with my mouth more than anything. I tell God how I feel, and I am real with Him. Now, as I look back on my original entries, I can see how far I have come in my journey.

Journaling should also be a big part of your new plan, but you will still need someone to walk along with you on your journey. I had a friend who became like the sister I never had. She is a Christian and had been walking the path for many years before I began on this journey. She allowed me to talk through what I was feeling and thinking. Since she knows the Lord, she helped me to focus on God's Word in processing my thoughts. She never told me what I was feeling was right or wrong, but always led me back to what the Bible said about the situation. She told me the truth in love (Eph. 4:15). Our conversations were not just about what I was facing; I allowed her to process her feelings as well. We were both going through different situations, so we helped each other to walk toward wholeness in our lives.

We need each other to make it through all the hurt, shame, pain, and guilt. God did not design us to be alone as Christians. Gal. 6:2 tells us to carry each other's burdens. We are to help one another and do good to each other (Heb. 13:16.)

You will have people in your life with whom you want to share what you are working through. I caution you to be careful what you share and with whom. People have different levels of input in your life. Some people we know on a superficial level, and they will not be able to help you in your walk. Just because you know someone's name does not mean you know them. There are others you have a relationship with who may be sympathetic to your situation, but they may not be equipped to help you because they want to speak negative thoughts about the people who hurt you. They love and care for you, but they will hinder your progress. You don't need people around you to help you do that; you can do that on your own. God sent my spiritual sister to me. We were not friends before that. I knew her through her sister, who had gone home to be with the Lord a few years before we got to know each other. We attended the same church but did not hang out together. We ran into each other about a year before my separation. We talked on occasion, and I saw her at church.

When I made the decision that I was going to leave the relationship, I told God I needed help because I was doing this alone. I had no family or friends to support me. God led me to call her. I called her and asked her to pray for me to clearly hear God's will for my life. She had been walking with God much longer than I had. After that, we talked every day for hours. We helped each other, comforted each other, valued each other, and prayed together. Prov. 27:17 states that iron sharpens iron, so one person sharpens another. Don't be discouraged if you do not know who that person will be right now. It may be someone you always thought it would be, or it could be a new person you barely know. Ask the Holy Spirit for discernment in seeking the person on assignment to assist you in your journey. God is no respecter of persons (Acts 10:34). What He did for me, He will do for you. He will not leave you out there on your own (Heb. 13:5). While you are waiting for an answer, journal, stay positive, pray, and thank God for bringing you this far (1 Thessalonians 5:16-18).

1 John 4:16-17 tells us that God is love and we should grow in love to face God with confidence. It's hard to love like God, though I'm not saying that we can't do it, because God says we can. But it's not easy.

1 Cor. 13:4-8 states that love is the only thing that will last forever. Too often, for most of us, love the way we believe it should be is short-lived. We love based on how we feel or what someone may do for us. When you love someone, you put your heart and head on the line. You open yourself up to being damaged by someone.

We hear it in movies all the time when a character professes that he or she cannot live without the other character. I don't know about you, but I think that is a lot of pressure to put on someone to be someone's everything. We are not called to be anyone's everything. That's God's job. He is the only one who has the capacity to be everyone's everything. It's too much to ask of a person or something you may have turned into an idol. I made the mistake of making people my everything, then held them to a standard impossible for them to keep. Then I blamed them for not being able to live up to a standard they never agreed to uphold. As you move toward creating your new normal, remind yourself that only God can be your everything. Anything else puts unrealistic pressure on yourself and others.

It takes courage to love someone. It doesn't matter who it is. Whether it's your parents, spouse, sibling, kid, or a friend, whomever it is you open yourself up for heartbreak, you give your mind and your heart to another and hope they will reciprocate. Sometimes it works out, but too often it does not. Love requires trust, too. You must be brave to trust. When you have been betrayed by someone you love, your bravery and trust buttons get broken. The courage meter is damaged. Like a broken refrigerator, everything that you put in your brokenness spoils. If you don't get yourself repaired, your love, trust, bravery, and courage will go bad and rot. Since you are not a refrigerator specialist, you will need a repair person to come in who is authorized to fix you. Jesus is the only one authorized to repair your brokenness. The Bible is the life manual to help you get the broken parts fixed. It is up to you to let

Jesus get the Word into your life. Through the Holy Spirit, I learned to trust again because He taught me discernment. He taught me how to love through unshakeable faith and gave me knowledge of Him so that I could believe that I will receive, and when I ask for the wisdom I need, He will provide it (James 1:5).

A plan for your new life must include dealing with relationships. There may be some relationships that need to be reassessed before moving forward with that person. Other relationships may need to be severed. If you are trying to rebuild a relationship, you don't get to decide the time frame regarding how long the person should take to forgive you if you are the person who caused the injury. Realize that person may or may not forgive you. He or she may want to hold on to the hurt. You need to be careful that you don't get into condemnation about someone who may or may not have the capacity or desire to forgive you. Just because you are ready to be forgiven does not mean the other person will be ready to forgive you. Prov. 18:19 says that it is easier to conquer a strong city than win back a friend you have offended. It may take time for you to rebuild a broken relationship. Humility will be the key for you to work with a person you have hurt. You need to know yourself well enough to make sure that you are not injured by the person with whom you are trying to build a relationship. Don't get yourself into trouble by allowing someone to hijack your emotions. Figure out a plan regarding how you can work with your loved one and guard your heart and your head.

I am working on rebuilding my relationships with family members after instances where we both hurt each other. There were times when I became so distraught after speaking with them that I could not talk. Their responses upset me, and I became too emotional. I wanted to maintain a connection, but I could not handle phone calls with them. I began to send notes with scriptures that I had prayed for my family and for me. I used the notes to express how much I loved and missed them. I sent messages of encouragement in the notes. I have not gotten responses back from them yet, but I still send notes now on occasion on colorful, playful cards. This is a small thing I can do that is manageable for me but communicates to my family that I am here when they are ready. There are times when I am writing a note that I get emotional but not out of control. I pray for these relationships every day. This works for me.

You need to find things that make you feel good about yourself, but at the same time communicate that you are trying to work toward rebuilding your relationship. There is no time limit regarding reestablishing relationships for you or the other person involved. It's a God job. When you are blessed to reconcile with the person, the relationship is not going to be the same. Reconciliation does not necessarily mean restoration, and it never will. You are different, and so are they. Build on what you have worked so hard to get, and don't look back on what did not work. You both have let go of the pain so that you can build on a healthy foundation. Be honest with one another and tell each other the truth in love (Eph. 4:15). It takes loving one another to trust one another. There will be times when your mind will want to go back to the pain. The enemy does not want you to be successful in your new relationship. The fear of trusting someone will come to your mind, so make sure to manage your triggers and go to God's Word. "Resist the devil and he will flee from you." (James 4:7).

Boundaries are crucial for your new plan. They will keep you on track in your new normal. You must establish boundaries for every aspect of your life. Boundaries keep your yeses as yes, and your no's as no. They help you decide how low you are willing to go and what you are willing to do in any situation. Think about what you can do before you set your limits. I set boundaries with my obligations and the commitments I have in place. Think about how much time it will take and if you can make the restraints on your time. If you are being asked to make a long-term commitment, think about whether it fits in with the other responsibilities you may have. As you create your boundaries, be specific. I made boundaries around my time, how much time I spent with whom, work, meetings, how far I was willing to travel, how much I am willing to pay for what, and my down time, among other things. At the same time, you need to be flexible. As we all know, life happens, and adjustments need to be made.

Creating boundaries takes time. You will have to think about all the things you do. It's going to surprise you when you list all of the commitments you have made. Don't make any decisions without thinking about them first. If you make a commitment, stick to it. Remember, you need to trust yourself. You need to honor what you say you will do. The other thing I want to say about this is that it is important that you don't let anyone pull you back to where you fought so hard to leave. There will be family and friends who will want to constantly remind you of all the wrong things you have done. If you are not careful, you will get back into guilt, which may allow people to put you back into a place you no longer belong. Guilt is a way to control and manipulate us. Watch for the "remember that time when you . . ." comments. Pay attention to what the people in your life lead you to think about.

What do you talk about when you communicate with family and friends? People are either helping you move forward, keeping you in the same spot, or pulling you back. It is not God's will for us to stay the same. We need to continue to progress to have our best life. The Bible says, "But without faith it is impossible to please him, for he that cometh to God must believe that he is, and that he is a rewarder of them that diligently seek him." (Heb.11:6)

It is so important to God that we use our faith to get our prayers heard and to receive our prayers. "Now faith is the substance of things hoped for, and the evidence of things not seen" (Heb.11:1).

It will take faith to begin walking your new path. There will be times when you feel as if you cannot take another step, but you must keep going, step by step, and day by day. It is a battle between your mind, will, and emotions against your faith and trust in God. I felt that I died daily with my thoughts and feelings that constantly told me I would not survive (1 Cor. 15:31). I came to the point where I knew God loved me, but I had to ask myself a question: "How much do I love you God?"

I love Him enough to allow Him to shape me and mold me so that I would be fit for His use (2 Tim. 2:21). God does not tell me all the steps to take before I take the first step. He does not give me everything at once. I have the faith I need to take the step without knowing where it will lead. Don't try to understand everything before you make the first move. That's what faith is. It's trusting without knowing and believing God has only the best planned for you (Jer. 29:11). There are things I asked God about and did not get an answer for. You must build your faith and trust that if you need to know, He will tell you.

The foundation of a building is the most important part of any structure. Compromise in the materials will weaken the foundation, putting the building in danger of instability. When the builder does not allow the concrete to dry and set properly or uses substandard materials, unwanted cracks and shrinkage will take place. The structure may not be as resistant to abrasions that come from wear and tear. Cracks form allowing water and other things to seep in and cause more damage. Soon the building may suffer damage with other systems such as plumbing or electricity. The building owner must work with the original contractor to determine if there are any warranties provided to correct mistakes. The owner may also consult with an attorney to determine if the contractor has further liability to correct other damage that took place because of the subpar work of the original contractor.

Our Lord God is our contractor. He has an unshakable builder named Jesus to help us lay down a solid foundation in our spirit. If we allow Him to, He will build within us a solid structure able to withstand the ebbs and flows of life. Using His Word and working in cooperation with the Holy Spirit, we will be capable of fending off the situations and circumstances that attempt to put cracks and holes in our foundation. Jesus told us that Satan comes to steal, kill, and destroy (John 10:10). But Jesus came so we may have life and have it more abundantly. Our part is to give Jesus permission to be not only our Savior from death, hell, and the grave, but to be Lord over our lives. If we see Jesus as our only security to escape hell, we will not be able to keep the cracks from becoming openings in our spirits that will affect our lives in ways that will weaken and compromise our foundation to its core. In John 16:33, Jesus tells us that we will have trouble, but He has overcome the world.

God is no respecter of persons; He has no favorites. What He does for one, He will do for another, but it may not be the same way or with the same result. It depends on how we receive Him. We are fully equipped with the whole armor of God (Eph. 6:11-18). It is up to each of us to allow the Holy Spirit to show us how to wield the armor. You can only fight at the level of God's Word you have in your spirit. Everything you need is in God's Word. Learn it, meditate on it, speak it out of your mouth. It will teach your hands to war and your fingers to fight (Ps. 144:1). Approach everything from the standpoint of victory.

Our lives are based on the decisions we make. They influence the people in our lives. Making a conscious choice to love like Jesus takes courage. It is scary to love someone knowing that person has the power to wreak havoc on our heart, but we do it anyway because we must. We are not wired to live a life without giving and receiving love. We must learn to really love without allowing ourselves to be damaged to the point of dysfunction. I caution you on something I learned about this on my journey: I lived so long with pain that I became immune to people mishandling me. It became normal for me. I was hypersensitive to people and suspicious of everyone for a while at the beginning of my journey. I wanted to protect myself from being hurt by anyone. I had to learn to handle the remnants of the hurt, pain, and fear I was working to conquer. As I kept meditating on God's Word, I asked God to give me wisdom and discernment about my interaction with people and the direction life was going for me. In other words, I had to develop my wisdom and discernment meter. We cannot live our lives making everyone a suspect because of our past. The purpose of your new normal is to allow it to be new. We need each other to exist, so it is critical to be unwavering with the boundaries you set and trust God to let you know who is there for you. That is how you can be at peace with whomever and whatever comes your way.

It's time to pull your thoughts and action plan together. You have a good start to your journey. Your thoughts, actions, and reflections will help you with your walk. This is not a one-and-done journey; you must put in the work to get the results you need to attain to be whole. Overcoming hurt, shame, condemnation, and fear takes time and determined effort, and there are pitfalls waiting along the way. The more self-aware you become, the more you will be able to dodge the fiery arrows that Satan will surely attempt to send your way. I gave my life to God late in life, but He knew I was coming. He protected me, provided for me, and kept me during my silly seasons. He gave me grace even when I didn't deserve it. I will be forever grateful for how God showed me mercy when I had no idea how much I needed it. He has done the same for you. Now it's your turn. Reach out and take his hand. Find the grace He has provided for you. A new life of love, forgiveness, and unshakable faith is waiting if you have the courage to reach for the promises God has for you.

Make sure to allow someone you trust to go with you on your journey. If you need to get outside counseling or therapy, don't be ashamed to get it. Ask God for discernment to help you determine who should go with you on your journey.

There is a difference between solitude and isolation. Jesus went away from the crowds to pray in solitude (Mark 1:35). Solitude is my most important form of self-care. I need to spend alone time with Jesus every day. Isolation is something different. It is where the devil kicks your teeth in by bombarding your mind with thoughts and feelings that hinder your progress and stop you in your tracks. We are not meant to walk through life alone. Do not lock people out of your life because you may get hurt. I may encounter someone who might hurt me again, but I have wisdom that I did not have before. I don't ignore God's discernment and knowledge as I did in my former days. Most importantly, I have the Holy Spirit and my faith is in God (Mark 11:22-25).

We are interconnected and need each other. Spend your time with the Lord and get connected with others who can help you stay on track in your journey. If you do not have a trusted person you can walk with, find support in your faith-based community or group. Use wisdom and discernment to decide what you should share. Ask God to send you someone struggling with their own walk along your way. As I learned in my walk, I shared with others who needed help. You will be surprised by how helping others will help you to be thankful for God's favor in your life. You may need to go over sections of your plan until it gets into your spirit and becomes part of who you are. Get what you need to be free, but also realize that it will be a spiritual fight to stay free (1 Tim. 6:12). Focus on what you have and be grateful for God's grace and mercy in your life. May God grant you peace that surpasses all understanding as you navigate your journey to create your new life (Phil. 4:7).

Game Plan for Your New Normal
Now It's Your Turn

If you have completed all the "Now It's Your Turn" sections, you are well on your way to your new normal. Here are some areas to address as you create the plan for your new life (be specific about the questions and how you will address them):

What does your prayer life look like?

What does your love walk look like?

Are you working on building or rebuilding relationships? What steps do you need to take?

How are you working out your fears, doubts, guilt, shame, and negative emotions?

Do you need professional help with processing your feelings and emotions? What type and from whom?

Who do you trust? Why?

What boundaries have you put in place for every aspect of your life?

What qualifications do you have for being in a relationship, both personal and professional?

How will you monitor your progress and what is your plan for continuing to grow?

Resources

The books listed on this page helped me in my walk. Find books and other resources that will help you in the areas that you need assistance.

John Bevere
Driven By Eternity: Making Your Life Count Today and Forever
The Bait of Satan
Under Cover: The Promise of Protection Under His Authority

Charles Capps
The Tongue: A Creative Force

James Clear
Atomic Habits: An Easy and Proven Way to Build Good Habits and Break Bad Ones

Henry Cloud and John Townsend
Boundaries

Kimm Crandall
Beloved Mess: God's Perfect Love for Your Imperfect Life

Dharius Daniels
Relational Intelligence: The People Skills You Need for the Life of Purpose You Want

Kenneth E. Hagin
How You Can Be Led by the Spirit of God
The Believer's Authority
What to Do When Faith Seems Weak and Victory Lost

Marilyn Hickey
Breaking Generational Curses: Overcome the Legacy of Sin in Your Family

Max Lucado
Facing Your Giants

Joyce Mayer
Battlefield of the Mind

Perry Stone
Fishing in the Sea of Forgetfulness: How "Sin Recall" and "Unforgiveness" Can Open a Door Allowing Spirits to Attack Believers

Scarlet Threads: How Women of Faith Can Save Their Children, Hedge in Their Families, and Help Change the Nation

The Judas Goat: How to Deal with False Friendships, Betrayals and the Temptation Not to Forgive

There's a Crack in Your Armor: Key Strategies to Stay Protected and Win Your Spiritual Battles

Joseph Umidi
Jesus the Master Coach: How the 100 Questions of Jesus Enable Anyone, Anywhere, Anytime to Have Life-Changing Interactions

Acknowledgments

I would like to thank God for giving his Son. Jesus, thank you for the sacrifice you made that allowed me to be delivered free. Thank you for dying my death. Holy Spirit, thank you for your advice, wisdom, guidance, and prompting to help me write this book. Without the Father, the Son, and the Holy Spirit this book would not exist. I would also like to acknowledge my friends and family who kept me encouraged and inspired me to share my story.

About the Author

Dr. Sharon Elaine has devoted her career to the education of children by assisting students and their families in navigating special education requirements. Amid a successful career as a teacher, educational leader, and special education advocate, she struggled in her personal life to find direction, balance, and self-worth. After her divorce, Sharon began to take a critical look at the lifelong relationships that contributed to her thoughts of inadequacy despite her professional success. Specifically, Sharon began to develop her relationship with God. She began to understand how her beliefs, thoughts, and actions contributed to her relationships and her divorce.

Beginning at the End: Finding Grace through Faith After Divorce is a result of a deep dive into the past experiences that have contributed to her life, and how having an intimate relationship with God has given her grace through finding victory.

www.ingramcontent.com/pod-product-compliance
Lightning Source LLC
Chambersburg PA
CBHW070722130626
46553CB00005B/2100

* 9 7 9 8 9 9 1 5 4 5 1 0 5 *